RE-ENGAGE!

America and the World after Bush

An Informed Citizen's Guide

Helena Cobban

LONDON AND NEW YORK

First published 2008 by Paradigm Publishers

Published 2016 by Routledge
2 Park Square, Milton Park, Abingdon, Oxon OX14 4RN
711 Third Avenue, New York, NY 10017, USA

Routledge is an imprint of the Taylor & Francis Group, an informa business

Copyright © 2008, Taylor & Francis.

All rights reserved. No part of this book may be reprinted or reproduced or utilised in any form or by any electronic, mechanical, or other means, now known or hereafter invented, including photocopying and recording, or in any information storage or retrieval system, without permission in writing from the publishers.

Notice:
Product or corporate names may be trademarks or registered trademarks, and are used only for identification and explanation without intent to infringe.

Library of Congress Cataloging-in-Publication Data applied for.

Designed and Typeset by Straight Creek Bookmakers.

ISBN 13: 978-1-59451-552-1 (pbk)
ISBN 13: 978-1-59451-551-4 (hbk)

Contents

Preface	*v*
1 America and the World after Bush	1
2 Traditional Security Challenges	17
3 Global Inequality	35
4 Strengthening Human Rights	53
5 Climate Change	69
6 Global Power Shifts	85
7 Rejoining the Rest of the World	101
Resources for Global Re-Engagement: Action and Topics Toolkits	*111*
Notes	*123*
Index	*127*
About the Author	*135*

Preface

The world we are living in today, which we will bequeath to coming generations, is one in which nations are more interdependent than ever. It is also more densely interconnected than ever before, thanks to the amazing (and still evolving) capabilities of the Internet. This new connectedness has already started to change the way people and governments deal with each other across international borders. For example, for the entire duration of U.S. military action in Iraq, from the bombings of the first day until today, American Internet users have been able to read vivid and nearly real-time accounts, written thoughtfully and often in excellent English by Iraqi bloggers, of what it is like to experience a massive military intervention like this one from the receiving end.

The power of the new media has the potential to democratize the discourse and decision making of the world in ways no one could imagine even a few years ago. I have been lucky to be part of this emerging global discourse. In early 2003, I started writing a blog, JustWorldNews, which soon acquired more than 10,000 readers from around the world. A subset of the readers coming from all seven continents takes part in the blog's online discussions in a way that provides new perspectives and builds new understanding among all of us.

But if today's new global connectedness is to help strengthen reasoned, democratic decision making, we will still need some "old media" to help us along. I have worked in the print media for more than thirty years, including a long career in print journalism, and have published many research articles along with six other books.

Books are still special. You can curl up with a book on a favorite chair. You can share it easily with a friend. It can sit quietly on a shelf, to be taken down and read with interest even decades after it is published.... But when I started discussing the idea for this book with the directors of Paradigm Publishers, we agreed we wanted it to be more special yet. We wanted it to be thought-provoking, broad, timely, accessible, and action-focused. It should be, we agreed, "a small book on a big subject," namely, the steps Americans should take and the ideas we need to think about as we try to mend our country's crisis-riven relationship with the rest of the world.

In writing the book, I have woven together many threads of my past experience, including the research I have done on a variety of international issues, my travels to dozens of countries to seek out the views of their citizens and officials, and my attempts to frame complex global topics in a clear way for nonspecialist readers in my columns in the *Christian Science Monitor*. I have drawn on my service on the Middle East Advisory Committee of Human Rights Watch and my twenty-year membership in the International Institute for Strategic Studies. I am also grounded in my ongoing experience as a member of the Quaker meeting (congregation) in my hometown of Charlottesville, Virginia.

For more than 300 years now, American Quakers, along with members of most other spiritual communities, have tried to act as a force for good in this land. From the days of William Penn and even before then, Quakers have tried to bring hope, dignity, and fairness to everyone here, including Native Americans and those who were enslaved for many generations. Most Quakers have tried to hold fast to the antiwar stance that we and the other historic "peace churches" view as a mainstay of the original Christian teachings. Quakers have tried, in many different ways, to work for an equitable, life-affirming social order in our country and in the world.

Members of my Quaker meeting gave me strong moral and spiritual support as I wrote this book on a tight deadline. One group read early drafts of the text with the valuable eyes of "concerned nonspecialists." They told me when my data or arguments seemed cockeyed or insufficient: my special thanks to them!

Readers who are not Quakers may wonder whether they should take seriously the arguments on war and peace of a person who is a convinced pacifist. My response—given both as a Quaker and a long-term researcher on strategic affairs—is that today pacifism is a more realistic and necessary approach to world affairs than ever before. Today, the potentially species-cidal challenges of global warming and nuclear proliferation hang over all of humanity. Meanwhile, our country's experience in Iraq has shown clearly that raw military power is not able, on its own, to resolve the thorny international security challenges we face today. Indeed, quite frequently military action can be counterproductive, creating many more enemies than it is able to "destroy."

Americans and the 6 billion humans who are not U.S. citizens need to be able to deploy a much broader range of policy instruments than just the megalethal tools of destruction that sit in our military stockpiles. We need to have a serious conversation about the utility or disutility of military power in the twenty-first-century world. Quakers, the members of the other historic peace churches, and Americans committed to nonviolent action have a significant contribution to make to this discussion. For example, the Quaker-based Friends Committee on National Legislation (FCNL), with which I am affiliated, has done groundbreaking work in researching the peaceful prevention of deadly conflict.

This book is another contribution to the discussion. It examines military questions along with the other main issues on today's global agenda, such as human rights and climate change, and shows how all these issues affect each other in today's interconnected world. I am grateful indeed to the editors at Paradigm Publishers for the commitment they have made to all aspects of this project—including the idea that the book should be both affordable and timely. Paradigm Vice President Jennifer Knerr proved to be an ideal editor: intelligent, sure-footed, and supportive. The whole Paradigm team has been efficient, helpful, and a delight to work with. Philip A. Schrodt and a number of anonymous reviewers provided helpful feedback on the text.

Some of my colleagues, friends, and family members gave various parts of the book an "expert" reading, and did so with admirable speed. Those kind souls include Ruth Greenspan Bell, Coralie Bryant, William B. Quandt, Tarek Rached, and Brantly Womack. My colleagues and friends at FCNL have given me a lot of encouragement with the project.

When I asked my blog readers for some specific input into the project, Christiane Roh of Lucerne, Switzerland, and others sent helpful suggestions. The original idea for the book grew out of a lengthy conversation I had with Paul D. Rogers of the Department of Peace Studies at the University of Bradford, UK, and is informed by the approach that he and coauthors Chris Abbott and John Sloboda used in their UK-focused book *Beyond Terror: The Truth about the Real Threats to Our World*. None of these people or anyone else can be blamed for the book's remaining shortcomings.

Helena Cobban

1

America and the World after Bush

More than ever today Americans, like the rest of humanity, need a functioning global system through which the world's peoples can face global challenges together.

—Kofi Annan, Former UN Secretary-General
and Nobel Peace Laureate

Our country's relationship with the rest of the world is damaged and is in dire need of healing. Even before the day in March 2003 when President George W. Bush launched the invasion of Iraq, there were already big problems in the relationship. But when he launched that invasion, without having obtained the backing of the United Nations and in open defiance of the preferences of most other countries, he set in motion a number of processes that have haunted our country and the world ever since.

Within Iraq, the U.S. military was easily able to topple a long-weakened Saddam Hussein. But the invasion also unleashed vast and unruly internal forces that made Iraq nearly ungovernable and kept the U.S. military stuck in the Iraqi quagmire for more than five years after March 2003. By the end of 2007 that engagement had cost the lives of more than 3,900 U.S. servicemembers and scores of thousands of Iraqis, most of them civilians. It consumed more than $450 billion of U.S. spending, financed largely by burdensome debt. It pummeled the reputation of the United States as a reliable, law-abiding player within the international community. It distracted considerable resources from the U.S.-led fight against Al-Qaeda in Afghanistan and Pakistan, and it stimulated the emergence of Al-Qaeda affiliates in many places where previously there had been none—including an extremely brutal affiliate in Iraq itself. Finally, the lengthy and draining U.S. engagement in Iraq distracted the attention of most Americans from other, deeper challenges in the international system, including shifts in the balance of global power, the challenge of climate change, and the mounting need for our country to strike a new kind of compact with the 6 billion of the world's people who are not American citizens.

Now, however, the Bush presidency is winding down. Our country will have a new chance to set things right—with Iraq, and in our relationship with the rest of the world. The future course of events in Iraq and the rest of the Persian Gulf is hard to predict. Box 1.1 outlines some of the prospects.

But this book is only a little about Iraq. It is mainly about the world-defining relationship the planet's 6 billion non-Americans have with our country, a land of just 300 million souls that for a decade after the fall of the Soviet Empire stood astride the world like a colossus but

> **Box 1.1 Prospects in Iraq and the Gulf**
>
> A wide variety of scenarios look possible for Iraq, the Persian Gulf region, and the broader Middle East over the years ahead. The most troubling is the prospect of a U.S. or Israeli military attack on Iran. Such an attack would almost certainly provoke sharp Iranian counterattacks against U.S. targets in Iraq and the rest of the region, and unleash further instability throughout the Middle East.
>
> Meanwhile, U.S. forces worldwide are now so thinly stretched that any acute security crisis in Pakistan or Afghanistan—or indeed, in Iraq itself—might force Washington to reduce U.S. troop levels in Iraq very swiftly indeed.
>
> Whatever happens in 2008, Iraq itself will likely present Bush's successor with tough choices. I have long argued for a U.S. troop withdrawal from Iraq that is total, speedy, orderly, and generous to the Iraqis, whom our country has harmed so grievously. A bi-level, UN-convened peace negotiation—with one level involving the major Iraqi political trends, and the other Iraq, its six neighbors, and the United States—probably offers the best chance that Iraqis can find a decent political agreement among themselves in the context of the U.S. pullout. The United States should participate constructively in a portion of these negotiations but let the United Nations actually run all of them.
>
> Whether this is the course adopted, or the U.S. drawdown from Iraq is more gradual or less orderly, there will almost certainly be a significant reduction in the U.S. troop level there before 2010. And over the next decade, the United States will likely have to reduce further the role it has played since 1970 as the dominant military power in the oil-rich Gulf region. Few people have given much thought to what will replace the current situation. The Gulf's coastal states—including, of course, Iran—share with the international community a strong interest in keeping the Gulf's sea lanes open and secure. A collaborative regional arrangement for maritime policing seems like the best option.

that now stands largely outside the global community like a distrusted stranger.

We should understand, though, that the decision Bush took to invade Iraq in 2003 was very consequential. It was a big-stakes roll of the dice in a strategically crucial part of the world. The now evident failure of that gamble will have consequences for the U.S. position in the world as great as those encountered by other world powers after they met strategic failures of similar magnitude. We could look, for example, at the diminution of global power suffered by Britain and France after the strategic failure of their campaign against Suez in 1956, or that suffered by the Soviet Union after its failure in Afghanistan in the 1980s.

I grew up in a Britain that, back in the 1950s and 1960s, was rapidly decolonizing. Almost every week, it seemed, in some distant land a ceremony was held in which Britain's Union Jack flag was brought down the flagpole and the insignia of a newly independent nation was raised. The new president or prime minister who took over the country was often a man who had previously been hounded or jailed on charges of "terrorism." Some Britons felt upset and betrayed to see the rapid dissolution of the once proud British Empire. Most did not. Most welcomed the end of imperial responsibilities, and turned eagerly to building new kinds of relationships with the newly independent powers.

I graduated in 1973 from Oxford, where the sons and daughters of many of those postcolonial leaders were my classmates. Soon after, I went to Beirut, Lebanon, to build a career as a foreign correspondent. From 1976 through 1981, I was a regional correspondent for the *Christian Science Monitor* and London's *Sunday Times*. I reported from prerevolutionary Iran and from the frontlines of both the Lebanese civil war and the big war that Saddam's Iraq launched on Iran in 1980. I covered many twists and turns in the Palestinian-Israeli issue, and reported on big political, diplomatic, and social developments in Egypt, Jordan, Syria, and elsewhere.

In 1982 I came to the United States. I was divorced and raising two young children alone. Continuing to work as a foreign correspondent seemed impossible, so I focused on other forms of writing about international issues. For seventeen years I contributed a regular column on global affairs to the *Christian Science Monitor*. (Over the years, it has dealt with all of the issues covered in this book and then some.) The six books I have published in the United States include four on Middle East issues, one on postconflict policies in Africa, and one on the role of moral leadership in building world peace. I have been a U.S. citizen since 1987.

I have continued to travel widely in connection with my work—interviewing political leaders, rights activists, survivors of political violence, and policy analysts on five continents. I have done hands-on work in Israeli-Arab conflict resolution, participated in conferences in many countries, and spoken at events in most of the states of the union. I'm a long-standing member of both the London-based International Institute for Strategic Studies and the Middle East Advisory Committee of Human Rights Watch. In early 2003 I started writing a blog, JustWorldNews.org. It now has thousands of readers around the world, some of whom contribute their own distinct perspectives to its online discussions. Those discussions, and others like them in today's blogosphere, can allow all of us to feel better connected with people around the world.

I have gone back to the United Kingdom at least once a year since I left as a young adult. I know that today, Britain is a self-confident and vibrant place. "Letting go" of the attempt to control distant others, as the United Kingdom did during my growing up years, can have very good effects for the country that does it reasonably well.

From "Control" to Global Inclusion

In recent years, and especially since the end of the Cold War, the United States has pursued a general approach toward many other nations that British authors Chris Abbott, Paul Roger, and John Sloboda have termed a *Control Paradigm*. In their book *Beyond Terror: The Truth about the Real Threats to Our World*, the authors described this approach as one of "attempting to maintain the status quo through military means and 'keeping the lid on' insecurity without addressing the root causes" (82).

The United States as a country never set out to create a globe-girdling empire. But it has had great influence on world affairs since 1945, when it established a unified set of rules—centered around the United Nations and two or three global financial institutions—to regulate international relations in the postwar world. Then, after the fall of the Soviet Union in the early 1990s, the United States and a few rich allies came easily to dominate the rule system created in 1945. The indirect form of control Washington thereby came to exercise over much of the world's economy had a huge impact on people in other countries, even if most Americans never saw those impacts. Most Americans did not particularly seek for the United States to "control" other countries—but nonetheless, in many important respects, it did just that.

The control paradigm as described by Abbott et al. is not a new phenomenon. However, all the colonial powers that followed it prior to World War II discovered, in one way or another, that it did not provide a workable model for their behavior after 1945. The post-1945 era has, after all, always been centrally defined by those portions of the UN Charter and the Universal Declaration of Human Rights that state unequivocally that the world's women and men are all endowed equally with human rights, including the rights to human dignity and self-governance.

When George W. Bush became president, he promised to adopt a "humble" posture in international affairs. But his administration's actions were far from humble! He firmly turned away from many international agreements and generally chose not to address the root causes of other nations' discontents. And he showed himself very ready to use military might to uphold U.S. power in the world.

Throughout most of his two terms in office Bush clung desperately to pursuit of the control paradigm in world affairs. But this choice did not help Americans to be safer or feel more "in control." On the contrary, it made us more isolated from the rest of the world than ever before, and hence in many ways far less secure. It also left many Americans feeling much more fearful about the future.

There are other ways to think of our role in the world that do not involve a self-defeating attempt to exercise control over most of it. Some Americans—in the post-Iraq period, as earlier—may be tempted to think that our country can manage best by turning inward and forgetting about the world outside. But in the twenty-first century, that is not a realistic option. Our country is so closely tied to the rest of the world through economic and personal links that dissolving those ties now seems quite undoable. Instead of isolationism, we need to find a way to stay in good and productive touch with the rest of the world—but one that is clearly different from a futile, continued pursuit of the control paradigm.

The best approach I can suggest is one I call *Global Inclusion.* This kind of inclusion would operate at a number of different levels, as described in Box 1.2.

A foreign policy of global inclusion would involve intelligent embrace of, rather than fear of, the currently shifting balances of global power. It would refocus our nation's energies on building global institutions able to meet the needs of both Americans and non-Americans. And it would unlock the tremendous new capabilities unleashed when human individuals or groups decide to work together on common problems rather than against each other.

Global inclusion is an approach that reflects the way most of us would hope that a well-run community would operate—but at the global level. In our own neighborhoods, if something threatening arises, such as reports of a burglar or rapist lurking in a strip of wooded parkland, few of us would respond by picking up a gun and going out alone to kill the miscreant. If everyone in the neighborhood felt entitled to do that, the casualty level could be huge! Instead, nearly all of us would feel a lot safer if we could rely on a capable community police force,

---

Box 1.2 What Would a Foreign Policy of Global Inclusion Involve?

1. Repairing our country's relationships with the other peoples and governments of the world.
2. Recommitting Washington to effective participation in the United Nations and the other international institutions from which it has become estranged.
3. Restating the historical U.S. commitment to the principle of human equality, and pursuing a foreign policy built on it.
4. Reaffirming our country's support of the principle of war avoidance, as spelled out in the UN Charter, and shifting our taxpayer dollars significantly away from instruments of war toward instruments of peace-building.
5. Joining the global movement that looks at strategic affairs through the people-centered lens of "human security" (see Box 2.2) rather than the traditional, government-centered lens of "national interest."
6. Working proactively to include in international decision-making those voices and views currently marginalized from it.

operating within the framework of the law and answerable to the whole community, to deal with the threat.

That is the approach global inclusion urges as all of the people in today's world, Americans and non-Americans, deal with the matters of even greater concern and danger that face us at the international level. Rather than seeing the world as a fearsome and mystifying place populated mainly by groups and individuals who wish us harm, global includers would see it as a single broad community that our country is fully a part of, a community in which responsibilities are equitably shared and community members all hold themselves accountable to each other. In response to a serious crisis like that of 9/11, global includers would focus not on ill-considered and unilateral military action but on police-type actions that aim at safeguarding the security of all members of the global community, and on building and maintaining the strong international coalitions for which such a policy calls.

From Threats to Challenges

Since 9/11, President Bush and other U.S. politicians and opinion leaders have put great emphasis on the many "threats" the United States faces in the international arena. In the months that followed 9/11, the U.S. public was treated to near daily warnings about "threat levels," and since then the language of threats has dominated nearly every national discussion of international issues.

By repeatedly reducing complex matters to the simplistic language of "threats," politicians and opinion leaders increased the fearfulness of the U.S. public. That language also increased the general sentiment among Americans that our country needed to act "forcefully" and defiantly reassert its independence from the constraints of an unsupportive world in order to eliminate all those threats. But then, when the Bush administration did act forcefully in Iraq (and indeed, in many of its military operations in Afghanistan in recent years), it increased, not decreased, the number of people ready to use violence against U.S. citizens.

How can we escape from this vicious circle?

One good way to start is to shift our mind-set from focusing on "threats," and to focus instead on the idea—and language—of "challenges." In general, if we look at something as a challenge rather than a threat, we can feel more self-confident about our ability to deal with it effectively. It helps, too, to recognize that this situation of feeling that our persons and our communities are insecure *is not one that is faced by Americans alone.* The challenge of vulnerability to capricious attack is one that many nations around the world share. In truth, Americans are far less vulnerable to terrorist or criminal violence than most other peoples around the world.

Once we start thinking about challenges, we can see plenty of them for all of humanity as we look around the world. Most of these global challenges are linked to each other in profound and complex ways. In this book, I will address them under the following headings:

Challenges of Military Security

Many U.S. citizens feel vulnerable to the possibility of further violent attacks on our homeland and to the prospect that additional hostile states or nonstate groups may acquire megalethal weapons and innovative ways to deliver them.

For decades now, our country's main response to external security challenges has been to use, or threaten to use, its own overwhelming military force. But in modern times military force alone seems—as in Iraq, and as the Soviet Union learned earlier in Afghanistan—to have lost its ability to intimidate opponents into submission. Meanwhile, today's high level of global connectivity allows everyone around the world to see vividly and in nearly real time the harmful impacts U.S. military actions have had on the residents of war zones. In the United States today, citizens cannot easily claim that "we didn't know" what has been done in our names in distant regions. And nearly everywhere else around the world, the readily available media record of events in Iraq has badly damaged our country's reputation.

In Chapter 2, I describe the alternative strategies a policy of global inclusion would suggest in security affairs. Most build on an approach called "human security," which maintains that security is most reliably ensured by (1) recognizing that all the world's peoples are interdependent on each other, and (2) building on that interdependence to address common problems—including the problem of insecurity—through common and cooperative efforts.

The Challenge of Global Inequality

At a global level, economic and social inequality have grown more acute over recent decades. A large proportion of the world's people lack the basic requirements of human flourishing—or even, in many cases, human survival. This matters to Americans. Since 1991 the United States has been the world's only superpower—or, as German writer Josef Joffe has described our role, the world's "überpower." Washington therefore received most of the blame for economic crises that befell many countries in Asia and Latin America in the 1990s—and it is largely responsible, too, for a world trade system that continues to this day to discriminate unfairly against producers in many or most low-income countries.

Many of the policies Washington has pursued in the international economic field are an affront to the principle of human equality as spelled out in the U.S. Declaration of Independence. In addition, the perpetuation of stark global inequalities exacerbates resentment against Americans and increases our vulnerability to violent attack. In Chapter 3 I describe changes we need to make in our aid and trade policies to level the world's economic playing field, and to start including in the global economy the hundreds of millions of the world's families currently excluded from any meaningful participation in it.

The Challenge of Human Rights Abuse

Too many states have failed to protect the rights of their citizens, or have even themselves badly abused their citizens' rights. These failings have sparked movements in the West advocating military invasions of abusive or otherwise dysfunctional countries in pursuit of human rights improvements. Even the Bush administration claimed that the invasion of Iraq had a strongly rights-related intention—long after the fact.

Today, we can see that the invasion failed to provide public security and other basic rights to the vast majority of Iraqi citizens. Indeed, war nearly always inflicts serious damage on civilians living near the war zone, and thus itself constitutes an infringement of their rights.

Americans will have to find a better way to meet the challenge of gross human rights abuses overseas than by launching military invasions. Chapter 4 will explore approaches global includers would pursue, including working more cooperatively with the rest of the international community on this issue, and—crucially—working to ensure that Washington improves its own rights record and thus regains some credibility in international discussions on rights questions.

Climate Change and Environmental Sustainability

Global warming is real, and the challenge it poses—to all of humanity—is urgent. The best panels of UN scientists have confirmed that over the past century the world's temperatures, sea levels, and concentrations of greenhouse gases have risen and that violent weather effects have become more frequent. They also found that human economic activities contributed significantly to those changes.[1]

Global warming has already started to undermine the livelihoods of millions of the world's people, stoking conflicts and sending waves of impoverished migrants across international borders and treacherous seas. Even with the best counterwarming policies imaginable, it will be decades before the warming can be slowed or stopped. Many people around the world have already taken keen notice of the relationship between global warming and increased global insecurity. In 2004 and again in 2007 the Norwegian Nobel Committee awarded the Nobel Peace Prize to recipients chosen specifically for their work on peace-related climate issues. Former vice president Al Gore was the most famous of those laureates.

The world's governments and peoples need to start working together—now!—to find a way to pursue the linked goals of sustainable development and human flourishing. Over the past 150 years, Americans have contributed disproportionately to the environmental stress and resource shortages that the world now faces. In 2001, our government pulled out of the Kyoto process that tried to find a cooperative global solution. The Kyoto process ends in 2012, so the negotiations leading up to 2012 will be crucial. Chapter 5 indicates ways the United States should re-engage with the effort to combat global warming and build a sustainable global economy for the decades ahead. This re-engagement is a vital part of global inclusion.

The Challenge of Shifting Power Balances

After the collapse of the Soviet Union the United States was clearly the dominant power in a world that rapidly became unified into a single economic system. However, in the early years of the present century—and acting within the rules of this global system—the European Union (EU) and China acquired considerable new economic weight, and national economies that had encountered serious problems in the late 1990s stabilized in Japan and Russia.

In the balance among the world's big powers, the main dimensions of strength traditionally have been seen as military power, economic power, human resources, and "soft power"—that is, reputational power. The United States clearly remains predominant in raw military power. But Bush's campaign in Iraq revealed that military power has become less effective than previously thought, and it inflicted great damage on our country's soft power and increased the U.S. national debt considerably. It is notable that this has been the first U.S. war ever to be financed almost wholly through debt, thus laying a heavy burden on future generations of Americans. In addition, much of that debt is held by foreigners. By mid-2007, China's central bank held more than $400 billion of U.S. federal debt—and Japan even more than that.

Chapter 6 charts some of these developments, the importance of which has been almost completely eclipsed by the attention Americans have (understandably) paid over recent years to the vexing topic of Iraq. Chapter 6 also shows, more encouragingly, that the institutions and norms established by a wiser generation of U.S. leaders back in 1945 still provide a helpful framework within which we can address today's shifting power balances in a nonviolent, inclusive, and constructive way.

Re-engaging with These Challenges and the World

The challenges we will face in a post-Bush world are many, and at one level they seem fairly complex. But they are all closely linked together. If, for example, we are able as Americans to help to reverse the inequities of the world economy, or to work well with other nations to stem global warming, then such actions will also help us repair our relationship with the rest of the world and thereby reduce the security challenge we face.

Also important to remember: we do not need to do any of these things alone. The vast majority of the world's other 6 billion people are eager for the United States to rejoin the world community on a sound and cooperative basis. I know that. Since 9/11 I have traveled to eighteen countries on five continents, and I have heard how deep the desire is among people in China, sub-Saharan Africa, the Muslim world, Europe, and elsewhere for the United States to put its relationship with the rest of the world back onto a healthy footing.

The decision whether we do so at this point is mainly ours. We all, as U.S. citizens, can play our part in talking through these issues and taking action on them—together with our friends and neighbors, in citizens' groups to which we belong, and with our elected representatives in government (see Box 1.3). The fear-mongering that underlay much of President Bush's approach to world affairs left many Americans feeling disempowered from being able to discuss global issues unless they could keep up with all the latest acronyms of "WMDs," the "IAEA," or "AQI." But these issues are not so terribly complicated. As I hope you will see in the chapters that follow, a basic understanding of human nature and what makes healthy communities tick can take you a long way toward understanding even the most pressing international issues.

Today, too, we are blessed with a number of excellent international institutions, most of them connected with the United Nations, that have already done a lot of the essential data gathering and analysis required for us to see what being part of a single global community really looks like. Today, the publications of such bodies as the UN Development Program let us understand much about the state of humanity at the beginning of the twenty-first century, and about our country's role in the broader human community. This book will have lots of tables and graphs I hope you'll find useful as well as suggestions for websites and other resources you can use to find out more.

But mainly I hope you'll feel able to use this information to re-engage—with your neighbors, with the nationwide discussion on these global issues, and with the rest of the world. Because by deciding to re-engage with the world, we really can change it, and the quality of our own lives, for the better.

Box 1.3 Connecting Local Efforts with Global Change

Chapters 2 through 6 of this book give more information about the U.S. relationship with the rest of the world in the areas of security and violence, global inequality, human rights, climate change, and global power balances. In nearly all these areas, there are actions we can take in our own homes and communities that have a real (even if small) effect on the global situation. For example, we can actively seek de-escalatory ways to resolve any conflicts we encounter; we can seek out fair-trade goods and raise money for development groups working in low-income countries; and we can "reduce, reuse, and recycle" an increasing portion of our own possessions.

To multiply the effects of such actions, we can talk more about these issues with our families, neighbors, and the civic groups and congregations to which we belong, and exchange ideas for further action with them. But, as citizens of one of the world's most powerful nations, we need to extend our efforts a lot further, too. We should work to ensure that the actions of our government at all levels—local, state, and national—also push forward the crucial commitments to violence reduction, human equality, and basic fairness if we are to re-engage our country with the rest of the world in a constructive and sustainable way.

As part of this effort we constantly need to seek out, and work to understand and share, the waves of new information about our country's place in the world that today's technologies make available. Much of that information is available in user-friendly form for reading or sharing either online or as printouts, pamphlets, or books.

Later chapters of this book contain many examples of policy changes global includers should push for. The Resource section offers more information about the issues covered. It also has contact information for organizations doing good advocacy and informational work in these areas. For updates on the resources, discussion on the issues, and news about the book, check the website www.Re-engage.net or my personal website Justworldnews.org.

2

Traditional Security Challenges

Wars are poor chisels for carving out peaceful tomorrows.

—Martin Luther King, Jr.

Compared with most other countries around the world, the United States enjoys a high degree of "structural" protection from external attack. We have broad, friendly oceans to our east and west and excellent relations with the two other countries on the North American continent. There are no hostile states anywhere near that give us reason to fear an attack from land or sea, either now or within the foreseeable future.

Regarding our vulnerability to other forms of military attack, whether launched with airplanes or long-distance missiles, only a handful of potentially hostile countries are capable of reaching our country in this way: Russia, China, Cuba, and possibly North Korea. Russia and China have long-standing agreements with Washington on conflict avoidance that have proven effective and sturdy over many decades. North Korea has recently entered into such an agreement. Cuba's ability to harm the United States (even if it intended to, which is highly questionable) has long been "contained" by our country's powerful ability to exert nuclear and other forms of military deterrence toward it. Any potential threat from Cuba could also be defused through diplomatic engagement—an approach our leaders have not tried in the past forty-plus years but certainly has become much more urgent now.

Between 1812, when the British Navy sailed up the Potomac and burned the White House, and September 11, 2001, the U.S. mainland did not come under attack from any significant foreign forces. (When Japan attacked Pearl Harbor in 1941, Hawaii was not part of the United States.) Few other countries have such a lengthy record of fundamental national security.

Perhaps the longtime big picture security our country enjoyed prior to 9/11 meant the attacks of that day caused a particularly deep shock to our national psyche. The attacks were outrageous. They capriciously inflicted death, mutilation, and the loss of loved ones on scores of thousands of Americans (and citizens of other countries present on that day, too.) However, the trauma of those attacks should not obscure the fact that, at the big picture level, our country remains extremely secure—especially if we compare our situation with that of most other countries around the world. Remembering this can give us the self-confidence we need to deal rationally and effectively with the other security challenges we face.

How, then, shall we start to fashion a rational response to the two principal security challenges our country faces: its vulnerability to terrorist attacks, and our potential vulnerability to the worldwide proliferation of weapons of mass destruction (WMDs)?

The Challenge of International Terrorism

President Bush's reaction to 9/11 was a classic control paradigm response. He used the military force of the United States and a small number of allies to invade two distant countries, declaring that the United States was thereby leading a "Global War on Terrorism" (GWOT). Between the two invasions he laid out his thinking on the role of U.S. military power in a key September 2002 document called the National Security Strategy. It said: "We will disrupt and destroy terrorist organizations by direct and continuous action using all the elements of national and international power. ... [We] will not hesitate to act alone, if necessary, to exercise our right of self-defense by acting preemptively against such terrorists, to prevent them from doing harm."[1]

Bush's hypermilitarized response to 9/11 proved strongly counterproductive. The U.S. State Department's figures for the number of terrorist attacks worldwide showed a huge increase in the years that followed (see Figure 2.1.)

There were a number of reasons why this happened:

- Terrorism, however vile, is still only a tactic. A country cannot declare war on a tactic, but does so on other specified countries (see Box 2.1); and wars end when either the opposing government surrenders or its armies have been wholly defeated. The GWOT, as a concept, was ill-defined and slippery. No one could tell when it might end, or even how to define final victory.
- The strong focus on "destroying" opponents gave the commanders of U.S. forces in Iraq and Afghanistan broad permission to destroy people and infrastructures that may or may not have

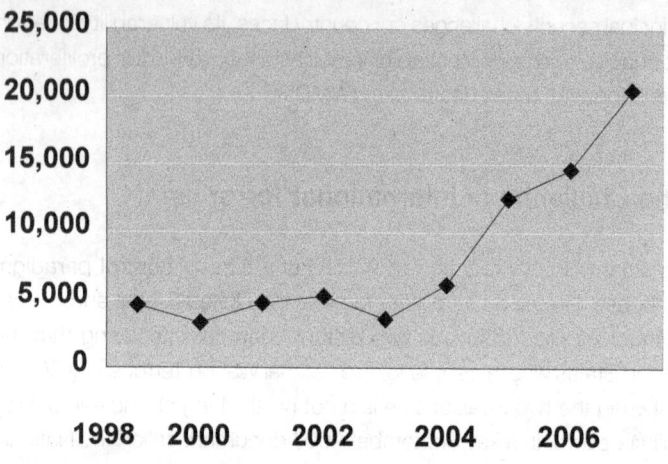

Figure 2.1 Worldwide Fatalities from Terrorist Attacks, 1998–2006[2]

constituted valid military targets. (Britain's military doctrine, by contrast, talks of "defeating" rather than "destroying" opponents.) U.S. forces used tactics like the bombardment of cities, extrajudicial killings, torture, and lengthy and widespread detentions without trial that violated international law and shocked the majority of humankind. These tactics alienated from the United States many people and countries that would otherwise have been our allies, and made finding and incapacitating the real terrorists harder.

- People and governments have long disagreed over the precise definition of terrorism. (The United Nations has helpfully defined it as "criminal acts intended or calculated to provoke a state of terror in the general public, a group of persons or particular persons for political purposes.")[3] In reality, most states' definitions of terrorism are biased and self-serving. The selective way the Bush administration defined terrorism proved divisive in international affairs and made Americans less, rather than more, secure.

How counterproductive did the invasions of Afghanistan and Iraq prove to be in the antiterror campaign? In Afghanistan, terrorist activity resumed on a serious scale soon after the 2001 invasion: in 2006, 749 terrorist incidents were reported there. And Iraq, which for some years before 2003 had not been a haven for terrorists, saw a huge eruption of new terrorist activity after the U.S. invasion: in 2006, the U.S. State

---

Box 2.1 Terrorists and Failed States

The events of 9/11 showed that there are terrorists of great ingenuity who can turn even mundane objects into weapons of great destructive power. We need to stay vigilant about securing airplanes, along with other potentially vulnerable facilities such as fuel depots, nuclear power plants, and emergency communications.

Our main focus, though, should be to work with others to prevent terror networks from becoming entrenched and beyond the reach of the law in the first place, as Al-Qaeda did in Afghanistan in the 1990s and as many terror groups did in Iraq after 2003. (You can read more on Afghanistan in Chapter 4.) One essential step in this campaign is to prevent the collapse of state institutions in deeply stressed and vulnerable countries.

In today's hyperlinked world, state failure anywhere puts all of humanity at risk. Using the analogy of neighborhood security introduced in Chapter 1, we can say that a failed state plays, at the global level, the same role a boarded-up drug house might play in an urban or suburban setting: a place where miscreants can gather in near impunity to plan further acts of violence against the broader community.

The Washington, D.C.–based Fund for Peace publishes an annual "Failed States Index." In 2007, its "top" candidates, in order, were Sudan, Iraq, Somalia, Zimbabwe, and Chad. Afghanistan was number eight. Iraq, Somalia, and Afghanistan have all seen recent military interventions by the United States or its allies.

Preventing the emergence of failed states and rebuilding them once they have failed are complex tasks that require commitment, funding, strong international coordination, and a deep understanding of the societies involved.

Department reported 6,630 terrorist incidents there, involving many thousands of fatalities.[4] The activities of U.S. troops in these countries inflamed their populations—and much of public opinion elsewhere, too. Estimates prepared in April 2006 and July 2007 by the U.S. director of national intelligence reportedly warned that the U.S. war in Iraq had acted as "a primary recruiting vehicle for Al-Qaeda."[5]

So how would a policy based on global inclusion respond to the challenge of terrorism? Firstly, it would define the main goals as *identifying, isolating, and incapacitating* global terror networks. Then, it would do the following:

1. *Recognize that these are largely political tasks, and approach them politically, not with brute force.* Any society can contain a small number of murderous psychopaths or sociopaths. But what allows individuals dedicated to terrorist violence to thrive and become entrenched in certain communities, as Al-Qaeda did in Afghanistan and parts of Pakistan in the 1990s, is that they find a broader community so alienated from the status quo that it condones the terrorists' anti–status quo stance and does not report them to the authorities. (Indeed, in Afghanistan, the Taliban government itself shared much of Al-Qaeda's opposition to the global status quo.) The key to incapacitating terror cells is to win over the broader community from condoning the terrorists' stance to opposing it. This can be achieved successfully only through smart political engagement.
2. *Focus on police work, not military force.* Most militaries are trained primarily to "destroy" the enemy and pay little heed to the social and political consequences of their actions. Instead of deploying the military we should deploy seasoned police investigators to cooperate intelligently and fully with their counterparts elsewhere—and to do so strictly within the framework of international law.
3. *Understand the difference between movements linked to local communities with identifiable grievances, and those that, like Al-Qaeda, are rootless and nihilistic.* Work to isolate the latter kinds of groups, but try to engage with the locally rooted movements, however distasteful some of their acts may seem—and do

not set the bar for inclusion unrealistically high. In the peace negotiations in South Africa and Northern Ireland the only condition for participants was that they abide by a ceasefire and prove their popular following in elections. They were not required to disarm their forces or change their political charters before peace talks opened. (Before each of those negotiations started, the two governments concerned had for many years denounced their opponents as "terrorists." Yes, even including Nelson Mandela.) Both those negotiations succeeded.

4. *Involve groups with demonstrated political support and understandable grievances in a peaceful political process as the best way to end conflict and instability.* In Northern Ireland, South Africa, and elsewhere the political inclusion of former opponents turned communities that formerly condoned insurgent violence strongly against it. In the United States, successive administrations vowed for a long time that they would "strike no deals" with those they labeled as terrorists. (In Iraq, that changed when U.S. commanders realized they needed to strike local deals with some insurgents. But they still lacked an effective plan for nationwide political inclusion there.) Meanwhile, the overly broad brush with which Washington has labeled numerous groups around the world as terror groups and therefore disqualified from political inclusion left the United States isolated from much of Middle Eastern society.

5. *Be even-handed in our opposition to all violence and antihumane intimidation.* If we want to isolate and incapacitate terrorists, we need to work with broad publics in the Middle East and worldwide. When these publics see the United States itself using excessive violence, or being selective in its denunciations of violence by others, that seriously undercuts our ability to win their support.

The Challenge of Weapons Proliferation

Since the end of the Cold War, our country's leaders have tried to justify a large portion of our supersized military budget by referring to

> **Box 2.2 What about the Threat from Dirty Bombs?**
>
> Regardless of the best efforts governments pursue to prevent the establishment of terrorist networks, there will remain some risk from alienated groups willing to mount terror-inducing WMD attacks against population centers. Some countries already have suffered such attacks. In Japan, in 1995, the Aum Shinrikyo cult attacked Tokyo subway trains with deadly Sarin gas. That incident killed "only" twelve people, but it sowed widespread panic.
>
> Recently there has been concern that terrorists might use a "dirty bomb"—that is, a conventional (non-nuclear) bomb that has radiological components packed around it. This is also called a Radiological Dispersal Device (RDD). Experts stress that an RDD is not the same as a nuclear bomb. Casualties from an RDD would be significantly fewer in number than those resulting from a nuclear bomb.
>
> The wide use of radiation in medicine, food processing, and other endeavors today means that all governments must carefully monitor the security of radiation devices used in their countries. (Spent fuel rods from nuclear power stations are another concern—see Chapter 5.) Effective governmental regulatory work and preventing state failure wherever it threatens will provide our best defense against terrorists with "dirty bombs."

the threat the United States faces from the proliferation of WMDs in the hands of hostile or potentially hostile others. The invasion of Iraq was justified primarily in terms of the threat Saddam Hussein's alleged WMD arsenal posed to world peace.

WMDs is a category that lumps together nuclear weapons, chemical weapons, and biological weapons. All these types of weapons are cause for concern, but nuclear weapons are much more lethal than either chemical or biological weapons. The use of the catch-all term *WMDs* handily fudges that distinction.

The large amount of discussion in the United States in recent years about the "threat" from WMDs has meanwhile obscured two key facts about the current pattern of international insecurity:

1. Our country still has the world's most lethal nuclear-weapons arsenal. Unlike other big nuclear-armed states it has refused

to commit to "no first use" of nuclear weapons, and it has been more ready than any other country to issue thinly veiled threats that it would *use* its nuclear weapons rather than just keep them for backup "deterrence." In 2001, U.S. military planners even prepared the first ever plans for possible nuclear strikes against states that did not have nuclear weapons but that were feared to be trying to acquire unspecified forms of WMDs.[6]

2. At the other end of the scale, the types of weapons that actually kill and maim the greatest number of people in the world are small arms, which are currently estimated to kill around 300,000 people each year.[7] Our country has a significant share of the global small arms market.

People who study weapons proliferation make a useful distinction between vertical proliferation—that is, an increase in the size of each state's arsenal of dangerous weapons—and horizontal proliferation, the spread of those weapons to additional countries. Though these two dimensions are distinct, they are clearly linked. Every act of horizontal proliferation is also someone's act of vertical proliferation. And acts of vertical proliferation frequently motivate other states to upgrade their arsenals as well, thereby stimulating horizontal proliferation.

For the past forty years, the main way in which our country has sought to limit the horizontal spread of nuclear weapons has been through the internationally negotiated Nuclear Nonproliferation Treaty (NPT), which came into force in 1970. The United States, Russia, China, and the vast majority of the other states in the world are all members of the NPT, though joining it has always been voluntary.

The NPT laid different obligations on the five states that in 1970 had recognized nuclear weapons arsenals, and those that did not. The ones that did just "happened" to be the five permanent members of the UN Security Council (see Table 2.1).

The NPT succeeded in significantly slowing, though not halting, the horizontal spread of nuclear weapons. Three states that never joined the NPT—Israel, India, and Pakistan—have built and retained nuclear arsenals. North Korea was an NPT member but left the treaty in 2003,

Table 2.1 Nuclear Capabilities of the Five NPT "Recognized" Nuclear Weapons States, 2005

	Total Number of Nuclear Warheads	Number of "Strategic" (i.e., Long-Distance) Warheads	Number of Delivery Vehicles for Strategic Nuclear Warheads
Russia	c. 16,000	3,814	855
United States	c. 10,300	5,886	1,039
France	c. 350	288	132
United Kingdom	200	200	64
China	410	200	32

Source: Carnegie Endowment for International Peace, "Nuclear Weapons Stockpile Chart, July 2005", accessed 9/19/2007 at http://www.carnegieendowment.org/npp/index.cfm?fa=map&id=19238&prog=zgp&proj=znpp.

shortly before it produced a small number of rudimentary nuclear weapons. In early 2007, however, North Korea agreed to verifiably dismantle these weapons in return for international aid. Negotiations clearly seemed to work with North Korea, despite earlier accusations that President Kim Jong-Il was "a madman." Other states, including South Africa, Libya, and Ukraine, have dismantled their nuclear weapons programs and joined the NPT as non-nuclear states in return for fuller inclusion in the international system.

The NPT contains valuable provisions to counter the vertical proliferation of nuclear weapons, too. In Article 6, the United States, the other recognized nuclear weapons states, and the 180 other signatories of the NPT all solemnly promised "to pursue negotiations in good faith on ... cessation of the nuclear arms race at an early date and to nuclear disarmament, and on a treaty on general and complete disarmament under strict and effective international control."

The NPT was just one of many international agreements into which successive U.S. administrations entered in the years 1967–2003 with the aim of controlling and then reducing the size of the world's two biggest nuclear arsenals—ours, and that of the Soviets. Through those agreements the vertical proliferation of the world's two nuclear megaarsenals was successfully capped, and then reversed considerably. But neither the United States nor any of the four other nuclear weapons states recognized in the NPT have ever made a serious, sustained effort to work for goals of nuclear disarmament and "general and complete" disarmament stated in Article 6. It is time they did!

The NPT may not have been perfect. But it and the other arms control agreements of the past forty years helped to control and decrease the otherwise terrifying tensions of the Cold War. And the relationships built up through those negotiations then helped bring the Cold War to a basically orderly end. Those were invaluable achievements. In recent years, however, hawkish officials inside and outside the Bush administration continually have questioned the value of pursuing negotiated, treaty-based approaches to the challenge of weapons proliferation. Instead of "nonproliferation"—a term that denotes a negotiated, multilateral policy to reduce or reverse weapons proliferation—they talk about "counterproliferation," which refers to the use of unilateral military action to destroy sites that are allegedly associated with worrisome WMD programs.

Counterproliferation—not nonproliferation—is the approach the Bush administration was following when it attacked and invaded Iraq. It is also what the administration has threatened, on occasion, to do regarding Iran.

The Bush administration pursued unilateral programs in other parts of the nuclear agenda, too. It sought (1) to upgrade the U.S. nuclear arsenal, and (2) to build a globe-circling "ballistic missile defense system" aimed at destroying a large proportion of missiles aimed against the United States. Both projects destabilized the global strategic balance. The missile defense project undermines a crucial 1967 ban on the militarization of outer space and threatens to usher in a terrifying new period of "Space Wars."

Meantime, at the level of conventional weapons—that is, weapons other than WMDs—the United States has become far and away the greatest practitioner both of vertical and horizontal proliferation of those agents of destruction. Regarding its own (vertical) proliferation of conventional weapons, we should note that in 2005, U.S. military spending made up 41 percent of the world's total military spending. (Nearly all of U.S. weapons spending goes into conventional weapons, not nuclear weapons.) Figure 2.2 shows us this. It also shows that the United States has been spending considerably more *per head* of our population on military items than any other significant world power. (Those are the black diamonds on the chart, measured against its right axis.)

In early 2007, President Bush requested that, in the fiscal year 2008 budget (due to start in October 2007), Congress authorize a military budget totaling a stunning $643.9 billion. He meantime asked for just $10 billion for the many nonmilitary activities carried out around the world by the U.S. State Department. The disproportion was clear.

The relevant Senate committees did not do any better. The Foreign Relations Committee approved the State Department budget request very quickly. But the Armed Services Committee planned to *increase* the total FY2008 military spending to $647.5 billion! It also proposed increasing the size of the active duty army and marine corps to levels notably higher than those requested by the administration. These

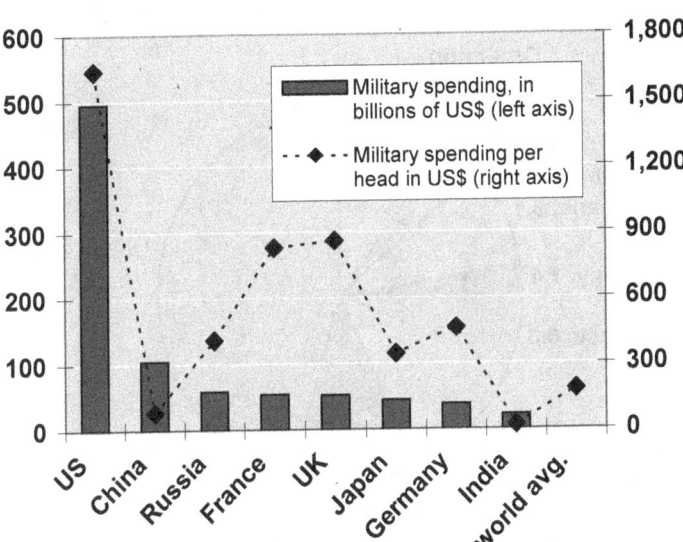

Figure 2.2 Military Spending by Some Nations, 2005[8]

troops and their counterparts in the navy and air force would, of course, continue to be equipped with weaponry that outranks that available to all other militaries in the world in terms of "reach," lethality—and, of course, expense.

The United States therefore appeared poised to remain by far the world's greatest vertical proliferator of conventional weaponry. It is quite certain that Washington's accelerated acquisition of new generations of weapons such as missile-firing drone airplanes and antisatellite weapons is already spurring other nations to do the same. It is equally certain that absent a real investment in international diplomacy and a more political approach to problem-solving, this military would achieve no more at the global level than the occupation force in Iraq was able to achieve in the years 2003 to 2007.

The United States has continued its excessive horizontal proliferation of conventional weapons, too. Figure 2.3 shows the shares that various arms-supplying powers have in the international arms market.

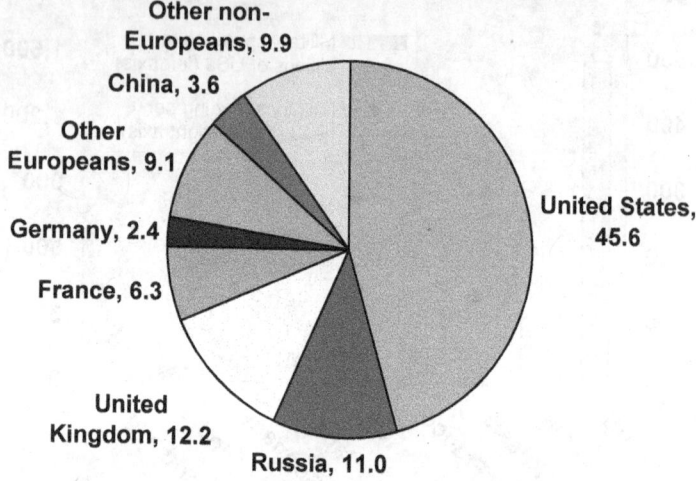

Figure 2.3 Countries' Shares of the International Arms-Transfer Market, 2005 (percent)[9]

Washington's "Arms R Us" approach to distributing weapons around the world has long had a strong Middle Eastern focus. In Iraq by 2007, U.S. military spokespeople were talking openly about how many different (and often competing) factions were by then being armed by the United States. At the broader regional level, in summer 2007 the administration proposed large new sales of advanced weaponry to Saudi Arabia and other oil-rich Arab countries, along with generous new arms donations to Israel and Egypt.

Washington's massive and destabilizing infusion of weapons into the Middle East and other strife-torn regions is another outcome of the militarized mind-set into which proponents of the control paradigm have fallen. But how would global includers deal more successfully with the challenge of global weapons proliferation?

Global includers would take to heart a few key facts. They would recognize that—especially in today's hyperlinked world!—one nation's security can never be built sustainably by increasing the insecurity of other nations or peoples. No one nation, however heavily armed, can "out-control" or dominate all the others. We U.S. citizens, like all the other peoples of the world, must realize that we depend for our long-term security and well-being on building strong, respectful *relationships* with other countries and their citizens, and sturdy and accountable *institutions* through which all the nations of the world can work together. That way we can hope to resolve our differences by peaceful means, and plan together for the flourishing of all the world's people.

Luckily, earlier generations of U.S. leaders recognized the need for those kinds of relationships and institutions. They built a strong framework for our country's diplomacy. They were visionary in founding the United Nations and establishing its antiviolent, values-based charter. (The charter, drafted in the last months of World War II, starts off thus: "We the peoples of the United Nations, determined to save succeeding generations from the scourge of war, which twice in our lifetime has brought untold sorrow to mankind.") Then, a later generation of U.S. leaders worked with dedication and vision to craft international arms control agreements like the NPT.

In the 1990s, however, it was not Americans but thinkers and policy-makers in other countries who most effectively pushed forward the thinking on how to build security in a now unified and increasingly interdependent world. These people developed a concept they called "human security"—an approach that puts the well-being of actual humans rather than the interests of states at the heart of what we mean by "security" (see Box 2.3).

The concept of human security has strongly influenced the work of forward-thinking governments like those of Norway and Canada, and of the specialized agencies that do invaluable work internationally under the auspices of the United Nations: the World Health Organization (WHO), the UN Children's Fund (UNICEF), the UN Development Program (UNDP), and so on. Sadly, though, the notion has had less influence on U.S. governmental policies. Some statements from U.S. leaders—including even President Bush's National Security Strategy document of 2002—have referred to the relationship between global inequalities and world peace, a topic I develop in the next chapter. But in practice, successive U.S. administrations have invested far more in using military force in a fruitless quest to retain "control" over

> ### Box 2.3 Human Security as Defined by the UN Development Programme
>
> The concept of security has for too long been interpreted narrowly: as security of territory from external aggression, or as protection of national interests in foreign policy, or as global security from the threat of a nuclear holocaust. It has been related more to nation-states than to people.... Forgotten were the legitimate concerns of ordinary people who sought security in their daily lives. For many of them, security symbolized protection from the threat of disease, hunger, unemployment, crime, social conflict, political repression, and environmental hazards....
>
> In the final analysis, human security is a child who did not die, a disease that did not spread, a job that was not cut, an ethnic tension that did not explode in violence, a dissident who was not silenced. Human security is not a concern with weapons—it is a concern with human life and dignity.
>
> The idea of human security, though simple, is likely to revolutionize society in the twenty-first century. A consideration of the basic concept of human security must focus on four of its essential characteristics:
>
> - Human security is a universal concern. It is relevant to people everywhere, in rich nations and poor....
> - The components of human security are interdependent. When the security of people is endangered anywhere in the world, all nations are likely to get involved....
> - Human security is easier to ensure through early prevention than later intervention. It is less costly to meet these needs upstream rather than downstream....
> - Human security is people-centered. It is concerned with how people live and breathe in a society, how freely they exercise their many choices, how much access they have to market and social opportunities—and whether they live in conflict or in peace.[10]

various aspects of world affairs than in implementing the concept of human security.

A policy of global inclusion would (re-)connect us with the rest of humanity by embracing the "human" approach to security, which can certainly help guide our thinking both on weapons proliferation and the challenge of terrorism. Regarding weapons proliferation, we need to understand that when Washington pours money into increasing the size or technological level of U.S. forces, it does not do so either in a national or an international void. A choice to do this inevitably imposes opportunity costs—whether on what we can do with our current budget, or by burdening future generations with high debt. It also has a big effect on the motivation and thinking of other people, and can easily make international problems more rather than less intractable. The emphasis that human security thinking places on the interdependence of all the world's peoples in the security realm is extremely relevant in this regard.

Concerning weapons proliferation in general, global includers would use the principles of human security and push for policies such as:

1. *Reinstate policies based on the cooperative, negotiated approach of nonproliferation,* and end policies using the unilateralist, militarized approach of counterproliferation.
2. *Freeze plans to increase the total size of the U.S. armed forces* or to develop new generations of U.S. nuclear weapons, pending completion of a thoroughgoing national consultation on how U.S. citizens want to organize our relationship with the other peoples of the world.
3. *Convene that consultation in the form of a National Commission on the U.S. Role in the World* that would make far-reaching recommendations about issues such as righting the current imbalance between military funding and funding for diplomacy; ways the United States can strengthen its own and UN capacities in conflict prevention and peacemaking; how to ramp down the size of all countries' arsenals of both nuclear and non-nuclear weapons; and conversion of factories from military to civilian-related production.
4. *Strengthen existing international institutions* in the fields of nonproliferation, arms control, and disarmament, such as the International Atomic Energy Agency (IAEA), the Organization for the Prohibition of Chemical Weapons, and the Conference on Disarmament. In North Korea, the IAEA discovered that the government had lied about its nuclear program. In Iraq, in the

1990s, the IAEA and parallel UN monitoring bodies oversaw the destruction of all existing WMDs and the dismantling of that country's nuclear program.
5. *Sign the Comprehensive Test Ban Treaty and the Anti–Land Mine Treaty,* and join other international movements toward the regulation of the international small arms market and the banning of cluster bombs.
6. *Convene a conference of the five recognized nuclear weapons states* to obtain (a) reaffirmation of the commitment they all made, under Article 6 of the NPT, to work toward a world free of nuclear weapons, and (b) agreement on concrete steps they will take toward attainment of this goal.

In January 2007, former secretaries of state Henry Kissinger and George Shultz, former defense secretary William Perry, and former senator Sam Nunn published an article calling for the nuclear "have" states to launch a new global initiative aimed at—finally!—implementing the Article 6 goal of a non-nuclear world. In June 2007, Nunn gave further details of the steps required, adding: "[T]he goal of a world free of nuclear weapons is like the top of a very tall mountain. It is tempting and easy to say: 'We can't get there from here.' It is true that today in our troubled world we can't see the top of the mountain. But we can see that we are heading down—not up. We can see that we must turn around, that we must take paths leading to higher ground."[11] Global includers would work hard to identify, help fashion, and then pursue those higher paths.

3

Global Inequality

We have created a slavery-free world, a polio-free world, an apartheid-free world. Creating a poverty-free world would be greater than all these accomplishments while at the same time reinforcing them. This would be a world that we could all be proud to live in.

—Muhammad Yunus, Nobel Peace Laureate, 2006

In spring of 2003, I was doing some research in Mozambique. A Mozambican colleague had brought together ten social activists in a provincial town to have a focus group discussion on issues of postconflict peace-building. The director of a local human rights organization was hosting the group on the concrete patio outside his tiny, stand-alone office. First, though, he wanted to round up enough chairs: it took twenty minutes of going around to neighbors to borrow rickety (but treasured) plastic lawn chairs before we could proceed.... In 2006, when I convened a similar group in a displaced persons camp in Uganda, my hosts looked for some time for even one chair before I told them I would happily sit on the grass with the rest of them during our conversation.

How many chairs per person do most Americans have in our homes?

Of course, global inequality is not just a matter of chairs—though chairs can be a valued marker of human dignity and self-confidence. But global inequality is also a matter of families having enough food, safe drinking water, shelter, medical care, schooling, and basic public security to allow their members to survive and thrive, and the communities of which they are a part to flourish.

Too many people in today's world do not have access to these necessities. As Table 3.1 shows, in Mozambique 104 of every 1,000 live-born babies do not live to see their first birthday (that's the standard definition of "infant mortality"). In the United States, 7 of every 1,000 babies die within twelve months; in most European countries, the number is lower than that.

So in Mozambique, a baby born today can expect to live only 41.9 years if present conditions continue, whereas a baby born in the United States can expect to live for 77 years. The inequalities in today's global system have enormous, and often brutal, consequences for the 6.4 billion citizens of today's world.

Thoughtful analysts of social and political affairs have always pointed out that the existence of stark inequalities within any society is bad for the whole fabric of that society, not just for the individuals at the bottom of the heap. Most Americans have long recognized this as true—at least, at the local or national level. But since 1945, our country has

Table 3.1 Basic Wellness Indicators for Some Countries and Groupings, 2004

	Gross Domestic Product (GDP) Per Head in "International" $*	Total Population in Millions	Infant Mortality per 1,000 Live Births	Life Expectancy at Birth, in Years
United States	39,676	295	7	77.3
OECD countries*	27,571	1,165	10	77.6
World	8,833	6,389	53	67.0
China	5,896	1,308	26	71.5
India	3,139	1,087	62	63.1
Sub-Saharan Africa	1,946	690	103	46.1
Mozambique	1,237	19	104	41.9

Notes: The OECD (Organization for Economic Cooperation and Development) includes the United States and some thirty other rich countries. An international $ is a measure that takes into account the different purchasing power of a dollar in each country.

Source: Human Development Report 2006 (New York: UN Development Program, 2006), various tables.

stood astride a whole new kind of globalized society. Secretary of State George C. Marshall understood the dynamics of that change better than most people. In 1947, in the speech with which he launched the international aid plan that would afterward bear his name, he spelled out the close relationship between deep global inequalities and global instability.

In a warning that still rings true today, he also told his U.S. listeners that "the people of this country are distant from the troubled areas of the earth and it is hard for them to comprehend the plight and consequent reaction of the long-suffering peoples, and the effect of those reactions on their governments in connection with our efforts to promote peace in the world."

In 2005, our government spent $495.3 billion on the military. But it spent only $27.6 billion on international aid—and of that amount, nearly $7 billion went into the chaotic attempt to repair physical damage in Iraq that was itself mainly the result of the earlier U.S. military action there.[1] Just over $20 billion was available for aid to the whole of the rest of the world.

For several decades now, world leaders have agreed that it is reasonable to expect that rich countries should invest 0.7 percent of their yearly national income in overseas development aid. In March 2002, that goal was reaffirmed by the United States and other rich country governments at a key meeting in Monterrey, Mexico. Figure 3.1 provides a snapshot of how some rich countries actually performed on that promise, as of 2005.

As we can see, of those countries only the Netherlands, Sweden, and Norway lived up to the commitment made in Monterrey. The United States was one of the poorest performers, giving less than 0.25 percent of its national income as overseas aid that year.

It is true that simply throwing more dollars into the aid process in an unconsidered fashion may not change much—as we have seen in Iraq. But there are ways in which we can make sure our aid dollars are maximally effective, and within that context, yes, we certainly ought to increase our aid budget to—or above—the long-promised 0.7 percent of GDP. However, there are other, even more important, changes our country also needs to make in its *international trade policy* in order to help people in

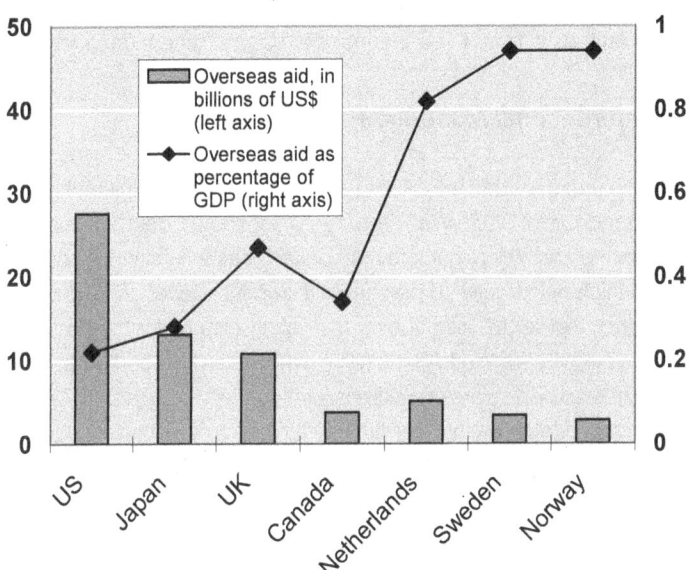

Figure 3.1 Overseas Aid Contributions of Some Rich Countries, 2005[2]

low-income countries. (We should remember, too, that almost no one, anywhere in the world, wants to live long-term on aid handouts.)

Global Inclusion and International Trade

The main cords that tie together today's globalized economy are those of trade and international finance, not aid. Just about all of the two hundred countries of the world are part of the world trade system. Most of this trade flows between the world's big, industrialized economies, but where it affects the smaller, more fragile economies of low-income countries, it often has a huge impact on them. Too often in recent years, that impact has been harmful.

To understand the impact our country's trade policy has on people in low-income countries, we need to understand a little about how this world economy in which we are living is governed, and our country's role in helping to control its governing institutions. In particular, we need to understand the "sucker punch" effect two key global institutions have visited on the citizens of low-income countries in recent decades.

The International Monetary Fund (IMF)

The IMF was set up by the Roosevelt and Truman administrations in the last months of World War II. As Figure 3.2 shows, decision-making at the IMF is easily dominated by the United States and its rich country allies, which hold nearly 70 percent of the voting power on its governing board. Figure 3.2 also shows the voting distribution in the sister body of the IMF, the World Bank (WB), which was formed at the same time. The two bodies are sometimes jointly called the "Bretton Woods institutions." Under a long-standing, informal agreement between the United States and the European Union, the United States has always been able to name the president of the World Bank, and the Europeans name the head of the IMF.

The IMF helps countries align their exchange rate and budgetary policies in a way that allows them to participate in the U.S.-dominated world trade system and to receive WB financing for development programs. The IMF gives large emergency loans that help governments weather serious financial crises. But these loans usually require the recipient governments to undertake what is called "structural adjustment" of their domestic economies. Structural adjustment has usually involved actions such as stopping subsidies to local economic sectors, cutting local health and welfare programs, and opening up internal markets to free access by foreign corporations.

IMF-imposed structural adjustment programs were widely blamed for the severe economic crises suffered by Argentina and several East Asian nations in 1998–1999, and they have been blamed by many Africans for the destruction of local agriculture and industries over the course of many years. Recently, some countries have vowed not to take any more IMF loans because of the harshness of its structural adjustment requirements, and the IMF has become a little less harsh in response. But it is still widely resented in the low- and medium-income worlds.

Figure 3.2 Voting Power in the World Bank (inner ring) and IMF (outer ring), 2007, Percent[3]

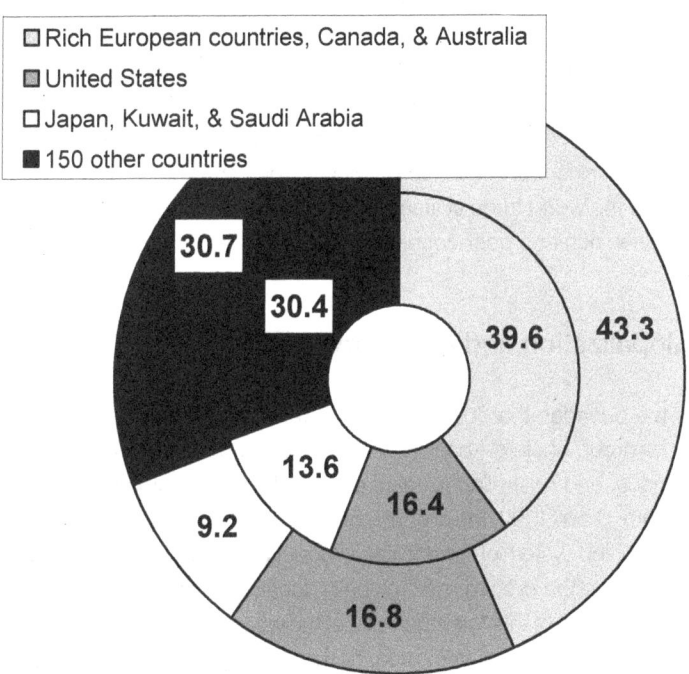

- ☐ Rich European countries, Canada, & Australia
- ▨ United States
- ☐ Japan, Kuwait, & Saudi Arabia
- ■ 150 other countries

The World Trade Organization (WTO)

The WTO links 150 governments that have all agreed (in theory) to rules that ban tariff barriers among them. It is the successor to an earlier intergovernmental body called the General Agreement on Tariffs and Trade (GATT). The United States, the other governments in the Americas, the EU states, China, and the West African and sub-Saharan African states are all members of the WTO. Russia and most other states that are not currently members are in the process of joining.

Decisions at the WTO are usually taken by consensus, but if it comes to votes, each country gets one. However, rich countries have far more ability than poor countries to lobby for their interests. One result: the United States, the EU, and Japan have all found ways to continue giving huge subsidies to their own farmers and other producers, although through the IMF these same countries have forced governments in low-income countries to dismantle the subsidies they once offered to their farmers and other producers of primary goods. The playing field of the world trade system certainly is not yet anywhere near level between rich and poor countries!

Globalization and Inequality

In the decades that followed World War II, the United States and a small group of allies—basically, the West European countries, Japan, Canada, and Australia—created a single, largely integrated economic system. Since 1990, the collapse of the Soviet Union and the entry into the U.S.-led system of most formerly Soviet countries, along with China, have made the system more globally dominant than ever before.

Advocates of this "globalization" of the world economy say that in an atmosphere of global free trade, all the world's countries will become richer. Critics note that this has not happened yet, and also that over the past few decades the disparities in wealth among the world's peoples have become more, not less, pronounced. WB economist Branko Milanovic looked at what happened to the economies of 130 sizable nations between 1978 and 2000. He found that five of them experienced what he called "upward economic mobility" in those years—but thirty-seven experienced "downward mobility." Plummeting toward, or staying in, the lowest of the four economic categories Milanovic identified were just about all the countries in sub-Saharan Africa, along with most countries in South Asia and South America. Staying in the top of his categories were the United States, the West European nations, Japan, Canada, Australia, and Saudi Arabia—exactly the same group that dominated the decision-making in the WB, the IMF, and the WTO during those years.[4]

Meanwhile, of course, there are also poor people in rich countries and wealthy people in poor countries. Figure 3.3 uses some of Milanovic's data to show the broad global distribution of wealth and poverty in 1998, the most recent year for which this complex collection of data has been compiled.

We in the United States, who occupy such a powerful position in the global economy as well as in world politics, now need to work urgently to cap and reduce the stark inequalities that exist within it. Rather than imagining that some version of "business as usual" in our international economic policy can achieve this, when Milanovic and many other researchers have shown clearly that it cannot, we need a much more imaginative and more thoroughgoing global New Deal. We need this for three reasons:

1. Right now, millions of people around the world are suffering—and dying—from the diseases of poverty, many of which can be prevented easily and affordably. Destitution kills people. It stokes conflict over resources that have become scarce. And

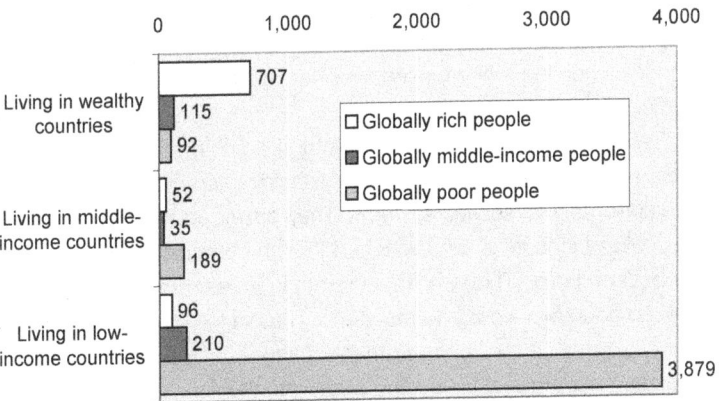

Figure 3.3 Income Distributions in the Global Economy, 1998 (in millions of persons)[5]

it prevents most women and men in the low-income countries from having the same opportunity to flourish that most of us in the United States and Europe now take for granted.
2. We could not ghettoize or wall off the effects of human poverty from our own country, even if we wanted to. Deeply impoverished societies become breeding grounds for diseases and forms of violence and mayhem that know no national boundaries.
3. The rich countries that dominate today's global economy can certainly afford the steps needed to allow low-income countries to thrive. And in today's hyperconnected global community there is now a good body of expertise that can tell us what works well in this regard. We need to seek out and listen carefully to the holders of this expertise.

So what kind of a global New Deal should U.S. citizens be pushing for? We need our government to adopt effective global antipoverty policies in the two fields, trade and aid.

Level the Playing Field in Trade

Under the rules established and enforced by the IMF and the WTO, countries around the world have been expected to dismantle any barriers they had to free trade. The declared aim was to create a "level playing field" on which low-cost producers could win bigger sales in the world market and thus increase their income. That, at least, was the promise held out to low-income countries in Africa, Asia, and Latin America when the IMF imposed structural adjustment on them in the 1990s.

The countries subjected to structural adjustment took difficult steps such as ending price support subsidies for local farmers and dismantling social service systems. They privatized many previously nationalized industries (and watched foreign corporations gobble up the best of them). They were assured that, in return, the rich, industrialized countries would do the same. Thus, a low-cost producer of raw cotton or cotton fabric from West Africa or Bangladesh might hope that her product would find a way into the rich world's booming textile markets and she could thereby start to build a decent life and livelihood for her family.

It did not work out that way. The governments in Europe, the United States, and Japan never did get around to abolishing either the tariffs with which they still protected many of their own industries, or the direct subsidies they gave to many of these producers. One well-researched recent study from Oxfam noted: "When developing countries export to rich country markets they face tariff barriers (i.e., taxes on imports) that are four times higher than those encountered by rich countries. Those barriers cost them *$100 billion a year—twice as much as they receive in aid.*"[6]

Regarding subsidies, the payments rich country governments have continued to make to our own farmers have had a particularly strong impact, wiping out the livelihoods of millions of farming families in the low-income world. The United States, Europe, and Japan have all been guilty of this. Between 1995 and 2005, the U.S. Department of Agriculture handed out *a total of $129.5 billion in crop-related subsidies to U.S. farmers.* In 2005 alone, it handed out $16.1 billion to 1.27 million U.S. farmers in directly crop-related subsidies.[7] (As noted earlier, in that year the whole U.S. overseas aid budget was $27.6 billion, of which nearly $7 billion went—mostly ineffectively—into Iraq.)

The general justification for our country's farm subsidies goes back to the 1930s, when President Franklin D. Roosevelt introduced visionary policies to help small U.S. farmers stay on their families' lands. That is still the justification, though these days the idea that the subsidies help struggling small farmers is largely a myth. Figure 3.4 shows how the crop subsidies were distributed in 2005.

Researchers from the Environmental Working Group calculated that the farmers in the top 5 percent of recipients—that is, families or businesses that already owned and farmed a large amount of land—got an average subsidy of $132,445 each! The 1.2 million much less wealthy farmers who made up the bottom 80 percent of the subsidy recipients got an average payout of less than $3,000.

Under the WTO rules governing fair world markets, neither the United States nor the European Union nor Japan should be giving any production subsidies to their farmers at all. In 2005, the WTO

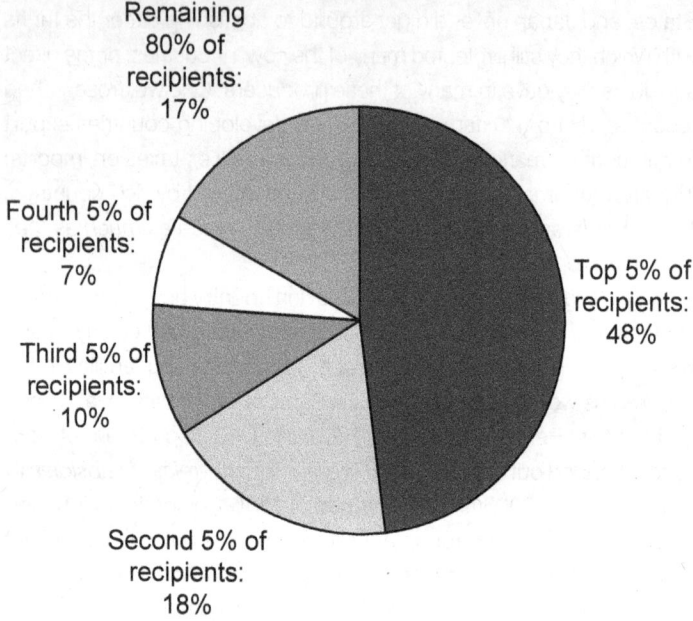

Figure 3.4 Who Got the $16.1 Billion in U.S. Farm Subsidies in 2005?[8]

ruled that the United States should stop subsidizing cotton farmers by September of that year, but in October 2007 a WTO compliance panel ruled that the United States had still failed to reform its cotton subsidies sufficiently to bring it into compliance.[9] The political and economic clout the United States—like the EU and Japan—has within the WTO has, until now, allowed these countries' unfairly damaging agricultural subsidies to stay in place.

In December 2005, business journalist G. Pascal Zachary published an excellent investigation into the U.S. cotton subsidies and the political clout of the big cotton farmers' lobby, the National Cotton Council. He noted the anomaly that corporations in U.S. high-tech industries have enjoyed no special protection from the government in the form either of subsidies or tariff barriers—but those businesses seem to thrive.

So why should cotton be any different? (He also included revealing interviews with people in the U.S. organic farming and environmental movements who voiced their own strong criticisms of the cotton subsidy program.)[10]

The cotton subsidies seemingly were not about to be cut off anytime soon. In 2007, the administration and Congress worked together on a new five-year farm bill. An information sheet from the House Agriculture Committee crowed that the bill would preserve and increase subsidies on a wide range of crops, including cotton. It also noted that the bill would impose a "hard cap" on the annual income of any individual who could receive farm program payments—at the level of $1 million. Clearly, this bill was *not* about preserving the small family farm! Indeed, by continuing to favor large producers, it continued a long process whereby federal subsidies had aided the consolidation of big agribusiness, often at the expense of small and organic producers.

Cutting off U.S. subsidies to farmers or other protected economic sectors may not be easy. Some of the affected communities may need help to adapt. But the federal and state governments can certainly find ways to help distressed communities that do not involve shoveling taxpayer dollars into the pockets of large producers, and that would enable us to deal with farmers and other producers from around the world in a fair-minded way. If we truly want to build a more secure world and to help the millions of families in low-income countries who have been damaged badly by our producer subsidies in the past, we will need to do this. We will also have to work hard to persuade the EU and Japan, which have similarly harmful policies in place, to be equally fair-minded. That is the kind of leadership that a policy of global inclusion, and a global New Deal, will require.

Aid Wisely

The same Oxfam study cited above argued persuasively that although action to make the world trade system truly fair is crucial, rich countries will still need to provide well-targeted aid to low-income countries for some years to come. It noted: "Aid can play a critical role in enabling poor people to benefit from trade, notably by supporting investments in health and education services and economic infrastructure."[11]

Here are the approaches we ought to use to revitalize our overseas aid programs. We should:

- *Follow through on our government's commitment to contribute 0.7 percent of our GDP to overseas aid.*
- *Build on the existing knowledge bases and institutions* in the aid-receiving countries and the international development community. We don't need to reinvent the wheel. Many people in aid-receiving countries have considerable experience in addressing their own development challenges. The UN specialized agencies and experienced nongovernmental agencies like Oxfam or Save the Children have great expertise. (Such organizations were responsible for most of the successes of the "Green Revolution" that increased agricultural productivity in many low-income countries from the late 1940s through the 1960s.) U.S. policy-makers need to work closely with such experts, wherever they are—and to listen carefully to their advice.
- *Focus on strengthening the public environment in the poverty-stressed parts of the world* in the same way the New Deal or Lyndon Johnson's Great Society programs did within the United States. This means helping low-income countries strengthen long-term capabilities in public health, education, public security, and stable, accountable governance. (Our government's failure to focus on those goals in Iraq meant that billions of the tax dollars poured into aid programs there were, essentially, wasted.) Our government's aid commitments to low-income countries need to be long-term, predictable, and focused on building healthy, well-governed societies.
- *Untie the aid from constraints imposed for internal (U.S.) reasons.* Much of what our leaders describe as international aid could be better described as subsidies to U.S. producers and industries, since the aid in question is "tied"—that is,

made conditional on the receiving country buying products and services from U.S. vendors. This often results in projects ill-suited to the recipients' actual needs. Also, if a U.S. "aid" project involves sending low-income countries farm products or other goods heavily subsidized in the United States, that can depress the prices for similar products throughout the whole region to which they are shipped—and it harms large numbers of the region's farmers. The Organization for Economic Coordination and Development, of which our government is a part, recommends that 100 percent of overseas development aid be "untied." By 2006, the United Kingdom and three other donor countries had achieved that goal. The proportion of U.S. aid that was untied was a shockingly low 7 percent.[12]

- *Emphasize attainment of the UN Millennium Development Goals* (MDGs). Our country's aid policies are far too unilateral and far too "politicized." The shortcomings of that approach have been shown in Iraq and in many AIDS-stricken countries in Africa. In 2000, the world community came together and expressed its joint commitment to the MDGs (see Box 3.1). MGDs define a clear and internationally agreed-upon path by which low-income countries can achieve social and economic development. Our leaders should throw their weight wholeheartedly into the MDG effort—and we voters should demand that the United States reconnect with the rest of the world community in this important way.

- *Continue helping aid-receiving countries escape from burdensome international debt.* One item of good news in recent years has been that loan-providing countries wrote off much of the debt incurred by low-income countries in preceding decades. Earlier, throughout much of the 1990s, many low-income countries had to make higher debt repayments to lenders in rich countries than the amounts of new aid they were receiving, so there was actually a net outflow of funds from poor countries to rich countries! The debt forgiveness programs need to be continued. And our future aid to low-income countries should be given as outright grants, not loans.

Box 3.1 World "Millennium Development Goals"

In September 2000, the UN General Assembly adopted a set of eight practical goals, with eighteen associated and generally measurable targets, to try to focus global efforts on poverty reduction and human development. The baseline year for these Millennium Development Goals (MDGs) was projected backward to 1990, and the deadline defined for their achievement is 2015. We are more than halfway along the path now!

You can get more information about the MDGs from this UN website: http://www.un.org/millenniumgoals. These are the goals and targets:

Goal 1. Eradicate extreme poverty and hunger
Target 1: Reduce by half the proportion of people living on less than a dollar a day.

Target 2: Reduce by half the proportion of people who suffer from hunger.

Goal 2. Achieve universal primary education
Target 3: Ensure that all boys and girls complete a full course of primary schooling.

Goal 3. Promote gender equality and empower women
Target 4: Eliminate gender disparity in primary and secondary education preferably by 2005, and at all levels by 2015.

Goal 4. Reduce child mortality
Target 5: Reduce by two-thirds the mortality rate among children under five.

Goal 5. Improve maternal health
Target 6: Reduce by three-quarters the maternal mortality ratio.

Goal 6. Combat HIV/AIDS, malaria, and other diseases
Target 7: Halt and begin to reverse the spread of HIV/AIDS.

Target 8: Halt and begin to reverse the incidence of malaria and other major diseases.

Goal 7. Ensure environmental sustainability
Target 9: Integrate the principles of sustainable development into country policies and programs; reverse loss of environmental resources.

Target 10: Reduce by half the proportion of people without sustainable access to safe drinking water.

Target 11: Achieve significant improvement in the lives of at least 100 million slum dwellers by 2020.

> **Goal 8. Develop a global partnership for development**
> Target 12: Develop further an open, rule-based, predictable, nondiscriminatory trading and financial system. This includes a commitment to good governance, development, and poverty reduction—both nationally and internationally.
> Target 13: Address the special needs of the least developed countries. This includes the following: tariff- and quota-free access for least developed countries' exports; an enhanced program of debt relief for Heavily Indebted Poor Countries (HIPCs) and cancellation of official bilateral debt; and more generous Overseas Development Aid (ODA) for countries committed to poverty reduction.
> Target 14: Address the special needs of landlocked countries and small island developing states.
> Target 15: Deal comprehensively with the debt problems of developing countries through national and international measures in order to make debt sustainable in the long term.
> Target 16: In cooperation with developing countries, develop and implement strategies for decent and productive work for youth.
> Target 17: In cooperation with pharmaceutical companies, provide access to affordable essential drugs in developing countries.
> Target 18: In cooperation with the private sector, make available the benefits of new technologies, especially information and communications.

Poverty, Exclusion, and Inclusion

People who work on alleviating poverty, both within our own society and overseas, stress that poverty is a form of exclusion that has both economic and political dimensions. People battered by the effects of serious poverty (economic exclusion) find it hard to have an equal voice in decision-making (political exclusion), and people barred from equal access to the political sphere find it hard to take advantage of economic opportunities that would otherwise be available to them. This is true within our own states and communities, as was revealed most glaringly by the events sparked in New Orleans, the rest of Louisiana, and Mississippi by Hurricane Katrina. This close linkage between poverty and sociopolitical exclusion is even more evident within the new global community over which our country exercises such great sway.

In the sphere of global economics, our government has already moved a little way from the strongly unilateral kind of "control" approach it has continued to pursue in the military sphere. Over the decades since 1945, our government has built and sustained a number of international economic institutions in which other actors, and not just Washington, also hold important sway. But that dilution of U.S. control still only has been partial: thus far, only a small number of other high-income governments have been allowed to share the control. Now, it is time for a more thoroughgoing, more intentionally "Inclusive" reform of the international economic system. We need to start treating all trading partners, not just the rich ones, with equal fairness and respect. We need to follow through on promises to participate in a generous and effective aid program focused on the international community's MDGs. And we need to think seriously about how to make the institutions of world economic governance more transparent and more fully accountable to the whole world community. These are the outlines of the kind of global New Deal that a policy of global inclusion would require.

4

Strengthening Human Rights

The development of the ideal of freedom and its translation into the everyday life of the people in great areas of the earth is the product of the efforts of many peoples.... No one race and no one people can claim to have done all the work to achieve greater dignity for human beings and great freedom to develop human personality.

—Eleanor Roosevelt, founding chair of the UN Commission on Human Rights, 1948

Many Americans have long felt strongly connected to the other peoples of the world because of their concern for victims of human rights abuses overseas. I have been a member of Amnesty International for more than twenty years, and I have sat on the Middle East Advisory Committee of Human Rights Watch since 1992. I greatly admire the difference such groups have made—both by winning real improvements for vulnerable individuals in other countries, and by increasing the sense of connectedness and concern U.S. citizens feel for men, women, and children living in different countries around the world.

Working with rights groups like these is something many of today's global includers may have been doing for some time already, and should continue doing. But what should we be asking our government to do to respond to well-documented reports of rights abuses overseas? This issue is not a simple one, though the record of the U.S. intervention in Iraq since 2003 has made some aspects of it a lot clearer. We should remember that in 2002–2003, when President Bush was still building the case for the invasion, he received significant support for his plans from several people in the U.S. (and global) human rights movement, who argued that Saddam Hussein's human rights record gave the West cause enough to launch a war to oust Saddam from power. Most of those "liberal hawks" were considerably to the left of Bush, politically. Their condonement of the invasion significantly broadened the base of public support for a war that was actually being planned by the Bush administration for different, more geostrategic reasons.

After the invasion, it became clear that Bush's accusations about Saddam's WMDs and alleged links with Al-Qaeda had no merit. Bush then shifted his argument and focused instead on the considerable human rights improvement he claimed the invasion and occupation of Iraq had brought to the Iraqi people. But that claim turned out to have tragically little factual basis. In the five years following the invasion, more than 80,000 Iraqi civilians were killed by documented acts of direct violence. Additional scores (or even hundreds) of thousands died from undocumented acts of violence, infrastructural destruction, or other causes stemming from the social-political breakdown Iraq experienced under the U.S. occupation. Violence and intimidation forced some 4 million of the country's 27 million citizens to flee their homes, with some 2 million of those forced to flee the country altogether. And from late 2003 on, Iraq's highly educated women—who under Saddam had occupied leadership positions in many professions—found themselves increasingly shut out of the job market and forced to obey the dictates of conservative Muslim religious leaders. By early 2008, claims that the U.S. invasion and occupation had improved Iraqis' human rights had lost nearly all their credibility.

Significant claims about rights improvements have also been made about our country's invasion of Afghanistan. There, too, the invasion was justified at the time (October 2001) primarily in terms other than those related to human rights. After 9/11 Bush decided that he needed to use the U.S. military to dismantle both Al-Qaeda and the Taliban government that had given Osama bin Laden a safe haven in Afghanistan. But he also, from early on, justified the overthrow of the Taliban on "liberationist," human rights grounds. The rights record of the postinvasion regime in Afghanistan was more mixed than in Iraq, but it is clear that the United States and its allies have not done nearly enough to help improve the lives of the country's 32 million people (see Box 4.1).

After the failure of the military invasion to remake Iraq as a democratic, rights-respecting society, and the uncertain record of the parallel project in Afghanistan, global includers are left with a tough challenge (see Figure 4.1). What can we realistically ask our government to do to respond to well-documented reports of atrocious rights abuses overseas?

This challenge will continue to be a difficult and important one for many years ahead. Governments in places like Myanmar (Burma), Zimbabwe, and the Darfur region of Sudan will most likely continue to commit large-scale abuses against their citizens. In other countries such as the Democratic Republic of Congo (DRC) and parts of Pakistan, Somalia, or even Afghanistan, the central government may not hold much sway at all. When states fail, the ensuing fighting among warlords can be just as deadly as even the most repressive government. I lived through just such a situation when I was in Lebanon in the 1970s, working as a journalist and trying to raise my family there. I experienced at first hand the suffering inflicted on Lebanon's residents by state failure and the armed contestation among the country's warlords.

Box 4.1 The United States and Human Rights in Afghanistan

The postinvasion U.S. troop presence in Afghanistan has always had a lot more international support than the troop presence in Iraq. Also, there seems a better chance in Afghanistan than in Iraq that the United States and its partners can help to build a sustainable, rights-respecting order.

In a sense, we owe the Afghan people nothing less. In the 1980s, the CIA and its allies used Afghanistan as a key battleground against the Soviet Union. That proxy war devastated Afghanistan and sent millions of Afghans into exile. But after the Soviets were defeated, the United States walked away from the task of postwar reconstruction. The result was the rise, first, of abusive warlordism, and then, of the equally abusive Taliban and Al-Qaeda. Everyone suffered: Americans and, even more so, Afghans. This time, we should not walk away again.

But if the United States is to do any lasting good in Afghanistan, we will have to change Washington's policies. U.S. forces have been working on two quite different missions there. One has been to secure and help reconstruct various parts of the country through the Provincial Reconstruction Teams (PRTs). The other has been to use U.S. Special Forces to hunt suspected terrorists—often using lethal means. Three dozen other nations also have troops working with the PRTs, which have a clear mandate from the United Nations. Several of those governments—and the Afghan government itself—have complained bitterly that the U.S. terrorist hunters have used unacceptable levels of violence against Afghan civilians. That has increased Afghans' opposition to the national government and built more support for the Taliban, which was never destroyed completely, and perhaps cannot be.

Afghan president Hamid Karzai has asked the United States to use far less lethal force in his country. He has called for conciliatory policies toward both the Taliban and his big neighbor to the west, Iran. Our government should accede to those requests. We should also work energetically with Karzai and the United Nations to design—and, crucially, fund—a smart new social and political reconstruction plan for Afghanistan. The major decisions regarding that project, including whether to include the Taliban in it and how to deal with the wide resumption of opium cultivation, should be made by the Afghans, not Washington.

As of 2008, Afghanistan's rights record still looks abysmal, and it will be hard to win real improvements. Successful socioeconomic and political reconstruction remains essential if the Afghan people's lives are to improve—and also, to make the country inhospitable to international terrorists.

Strengthening Human Rights • 57

Figure 4.1 Rights Indicators for Various Countries (2004, unless otherwise noted)[1]

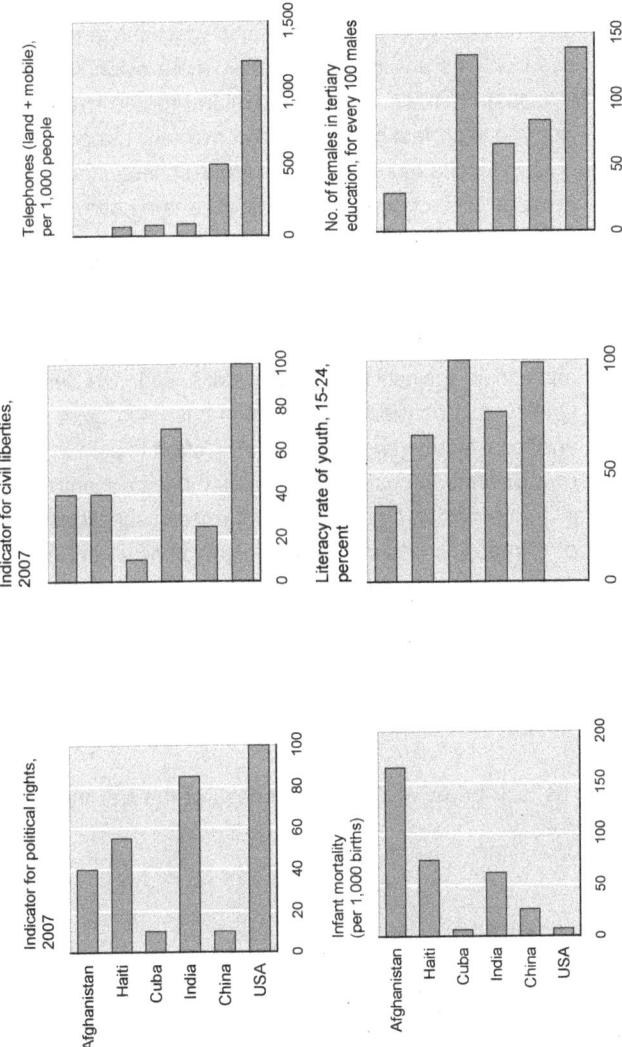

Note: Where no bars are shown, no data were available.

In recent years, our government has had four main kinds of responses to atrocities overseas:

1. It has sometimes used *military action* for primarily rights-related reasons (as opposed to occasions when those reasons were used only as an adjunct to other, more evidently "strategic" reasons). In 1993, President Clinton ordered military units in Somalia to protect humanitarian convoys by using military force against local warlords (with disastrous consequences). In 1999, because of his concern over rights abuses in Kosovo, he ordered the bombing of targets in Serbia.
2. Washington has more frequently imposed *economic sanctions*—that is, restrictions on trade or financial interactions—against offending governments, as in Myanmar, Sudan, and Zimbabwe; and earlier, against Cuba, South Africa, Iraq, and Serbia.
3. On several occasions, Washington has used *quiet diplomacy* and "constructive engagement" in an effort to persuade abusive governments to change their ways. It has frequently done this in connection with promises to lift existing sanctions (a carrot), or to impose sanctions (a stick). Sometimes, as in South Africa, these efforts have succeeded.
4. On numerous occasions, it has *done nothing*. On one occasion—Rwanda, in 1994—it did less than nothing: it quite shamefully *withdrew* essential political support from the UN rights protection operation that was already present on the ground there.

Let us look briefly at the effectiveness of the first three of these strategies.

Military Action

The temptation can seem great. Our country has poured a lot of money into building a large and technically sophisticated military (and pitifully little into building other, nonmilitary means for interacting with the rest of the world.) The technological advances of recent decades allowed military leaders to talk about "smart" weapons that could destroy a specified target halfway around the world, with almost no risk either to the civilians living nearby or to U.S. forces or their allies. The collapse of the Soviet Union in 1991 gave the U.S. military a lot more freedom to move its forces almost anywhere it pleased without fear of triggering a global war. And by the 1990s the idea that some wars could be thought of as "good" had come to be held by increasing numbers of Americans—including those who looked back at World War II through distinctly rose-colored spectacles. That made the idea of sending U.S. troops into battle for good, rights-related purposes in distant countries seem all the more doable, or even necessary.

The first attempt to do this in the post–Cold War world was in Somalia in 1993. That campaign was a damaging fiasco that left Somalia no better off. And it left President Clinton so wary of overseas troop engagements that during the Rwandan genocide of 1994, not only did he not send any U.S. troops to strengthen the UN force then present in Rwanda but he actually tried to *have the whole UN force pulled out,* for fear that if it stayed the U.S. military would get drawn into the fray.

The next attempts to use U.S. troops for rights-related purposes were in Bosnia in 1995 and Kosovo in 1999. In those cases the United States, working with its NATO allies, bombed Serbia to try to force it to make concessions in UN/NATO peace negotiations. Those operations met their goals in the short term, though it is possible that the goals could have been better met using other means. By 2008, however, large numbers of NATO and UN forces were *still* needed to keep the uncertain peace prevailing in both Bosnia and Kosovo. So military action still does not look like a reliable way to bring a clear and sustainable end to rights abuses overseas.

Now, after the debacle in Iraq and the troubling course of events in Afghanistan, the idea that U.S. military action can bring a decisive end to overseas rights abuses has lost much of its earlier appeal. There may still be some situations that call for international forces tough enough to do what the UN calls "peace enforcement." (That is different from peacekeeping, which is when lightly armed international forces deploy to monitor a preexisting ceasefire. Peace enforcement forces have heavier weapons and a broader mandate to use them.) But given the experience of the years since 1993 and the broad distrust with which much of the international community now views our government, it is probably best for everyone concerned if we seek to have the U.S. military participate in rights-related peace operations *only if we have a clear and broadly supported UN mandate.*

The best contribution the United States can make to UN-led peace operations usually will be in providing airlift, sealift, and other forms of logistical support. But our leaders need to tell the military to give up its present refusal to serve in UN missions under officers from other countries. Officers from many other countries have a lot more experience of running successful peace operations than U.S. officers have.

We should meanwhile also be *working hard to strengthen the many nonmilitary ways our country can intervene to help rebuild societies ravaged by atrocities.* Because of the cyclical nature of the conflicts in which most of today's atrocities are committed, helping countries rebuild successfully after past episodes of conflict is one of the best ways to prevent future atrocities. This involves many tasks in the human security agenda such as rebuilding livelihoods destroyed by the conflict; rebuilding political systems in a way that is inclusive and allows for the nonviolent resolution of differences; building justice systems and police forces accountable to the communities they serve; and building school systems that teach tolerance, critical thinking, and the importance of nonviolent problem-solving. Many countries in the Third World have good track records in such tasks—much better than our record in Iraq! We should give generous funds to countries such as Mozambique or South Africa to send advisors to Sudan or Congo to work on human security and political reform projects there.

Those tasks do all need money—though still only a tiny fraction of what our country's recent and ongoing military campaigns have cost. And if we meanwhile pursue the policies regarding trade and aid outlined in Chapter 3, focusing those efforts on the low-income regions in which most of today's atrocities are being committed, we can do much more to prevent the commission of future rights abuses than we could through any number of military interventions. But if the only tool Washington has invested serious amounts of money in creating is a military hammer, then it is most likely to carry on treating every problem like a nail. It is time for Congress to start funding a whole new *nonmilitary toolkit* for our country's engagements overseas.

Sanctions

Using economic sanctions to end human rights abuses overseas is complicated. For a long time, the main kinds of sanctions used were broad, and they affected mainly the poorest and most vulnerable members of society. More recently, policy-makers have tried to implement "smart" sanctions that target abusive decision-makers more closely but reduce the damage caused to vulnerable others. However, just as with bombs, sanctions can never be made completely smart in this way. The experience of most sanctions campaigns in recent years has been that they strengthened rather than weakened the ruling elites in the countries targeted.

We can learn a lot about what helps to make a sanction policy effective if we study the contrasts between the sanctions imposed against Iraq in the 1990s—which did not succeed in sparking the overthrow of Saddam Hussein's government there—and those imposed because of apartheid in South Africa a decade earlier, which worked. What made the difference?

1. The sanctions against South Africa were focused only on the government's human rights record, whereas those against Iraq were aimed primarily at persuading Saddam Hussein to dismantle his WMD programs. That was an important difference. In Iraq, the United Nations estimated that some 500,000 children died because of sanctions. (The sanctions regime barred Iraq from importing chlorine-based chemicals the U.S. and UK governments claimed could be used to make chemical weapons. But those chemicals were irreplaceable for water treatment. Iraq's water supplies became increasingly contaminated, and the children died.) In South Africa, by contrast, the

sanctions had no other purpose that interfered with the central, rights-related purpose of ending apartheid.
2. The sanctions against South Africa had the clear support of a large majority of the country's most discriminated-against people. True, those sanctions harmed the country's "black" and "colored" populations much more than they did the 12 percent of South Africans who were "white." The leaders of the African National Congress, which represented a strong majority of the country's people, understood that, but they still gave strong support to the sanctions. They judged (correctly) that the medium-term pain of the sanctions could help bring the long-term gain of ending apartheid. In Iraq, nearly all Iraqis, inside and outside the country, opposed the sanctions, and they blamed the United States, the United Kingdom, and the United Nations for the harms inflicted—not Saddam.
3. The sanctions against South Africa had the overwhelming support of the international community. It is true that the sanctions against Iraq were also set in place by the United Nations. But over the years, many in the international community came to judge that the United Nations was manipulated by the United States and the United Kingdom in a highly politicized way.
4. The Reagan administration combined its support for the sanctions against South Africa with a policy of constructive diplomatic engagement. That helped the all-white government find a graceful way to end apartheid and allowed all South Africans to start to work together to build a strong and rights-respecting country. In Iraq, neither Saddam nor the Iraqi people were ever offered a viable way out of the pain the sanctions caused, and the sanctions continued until the U.S.-led invasion of 2003.

This brief comparison offers pointers as to when we might expect economic sanctions to help end rights abuses in other countries. To be effective, such sanctions should:

- Be as closely targeted as possible on the decision-makers responsible for the abuses;

- Be linked to clear goals that relate only to human rights, and not to other, more geostrategic issues;
- Enjoy the clearly stated support of a large majority of the people whose rights we are seeking to ensure—who might, despite our best efforts, still be harmed by them;
- Enjoy broad international support; and
- Be linked to an intelligent diplomacy that pursues nonviolent, negotiated ways to achieve the stated rights goals.

Quiet Diplomacy

Box 4.2 sketches the main framework of the international human rights treaties in place today. Note that under international law, social and economic rights have a status equal to civil and political rights. Over the past thirty years, the two biggest leaps the world has seen in the realization of human rights occurred when (1) the Soviet Union and its

---

Box 4.2 Human Rights and Humanitarianism: Some Key Terms

The basic document of the modern rights movement is the Universal Declaration of Human Rights (UDHR), adopted by the UN General Assembly in 1948. It proclaimed the equality of all persons before the law, and stated that everyone has the right to due process, including a fair trial if accused.

Other, more substantive rights were spelled out in two later international covenants: one on civil and political rights (ICCPR), and one on economic and social rights (ICESR). U.S. politicians and rights activists have generally given more weight to the ICCPR, which covers rights such as the freedom of assembly, freedom to form political parties, and freedom of the press. The ICESR, which specifies rights to things such as jobs, housing, and health care, has gotten less attention. The United States has ratified the ICCPR but not the ICESR.

The UN General Assembly has also adopted other important human rights documents, including conventions on children's

box continues on next page

rights, women's rights, and antiracism. The United States has not ratified most of these. Generally, once a state ratifies one of these conventions, it implements it through its national legal system, not any international body.

International Humanitarian Law (IHL)

IHL, also called the "laws of war," was first codified in international treaties in the late nineteenth century. Today, the most important parts of IHL are the 1949 Geneva Conventions, which regulate how states behave once they are at war, but not the earlier decision to go to war. The Geneva Conventions set firm standards in areas such as the care of wounded soldiers, the treatment of prisoners of war, and the treatment of residents of war zones.

The United States is a full party to the Geneva Conventions and has incorporated its rules into the legal system run by the U.S. military. Most U.S. military lawyers strongly upheld these rules even when the Bush administration tried to undermine them.

The Switzerland-based International Committee of the Red Cross (ICRC) has special rights to oversee the implementation of the Geneva Conventions, including by visiting prisoners of war and by helping them communicate with their families. The ICRC does other specialized humanitarian work in war zones, too.

"Humanitarian Intervention"

Some people in the United States use this term to refer to certain kinds of war, though ICRC leaders and other humanitarian workers emphasize that wars, by their nature, always harm people and are therefore antihumanitarian. Also, "intervention" seems like a slippery euphemism for "war." (An intervention in a foreign country need not be military. It could also involve diplomatic work or the provision of much-needed material aid.)

We should call wars by their proper name, recognizing that they involve military action with potentially destructive consequences.

---

broader empire collapsed in a generally peaceful way, and hundreds of millions of people in Europe and Central Asia won their civil and political rights for the first time, and (2) the People's Republic of China emerged from the chaos of the Cultural Revolution, and more than a billion Chinese citizens saw an unprecedently rapid improvement in their social and economic rights.

In China, that large-scale rights improvement occurred with almost no intervention from outside governments. In the former Soviet Union, by contrast, the diplomacy pursued by the United States and other Western powers had significant influence on the transition. The Western governments achieved it primarily by having explicit human rights standards written into the text of the Helsinki Treaty, a 1975 agreement among the United States, Canada, the Soviet Union, and thirty-two countries from Eastern and Western Europe.

The Helsinki Treaty gave something to everyone. To the Soviets it gave valuable international recognition to the political borders its armies had established in Europe in 1945. To the Western states it gave assurance that the Soviets, like all other participating states, would "respect human rights and fundamental freedoms, including the freedom of thought, conscience, religion, or belief for all." Over the years after 1975, prodemocracy activists in Russia and other Eastern European states used the Helsinki language on rights to help protect the peaceful citizens' movements they were building in their own countries, and fourteen years later those movements peacefully pushed aside the Soviet-installed overlords in East Germany, Hungary, Poland, and the other Eastern European countries. The prodemocracy movement then triumphed in other parts of the Soviet Empire, and by 1993 it had triumphed within Russia itself.

All that vast transformation occurred without the West using any military force at all. The West had used some trade sanctions in its relations with the Soviets over the years, and it kept up the pressure on the Communist countries' economies by forcing them to compete in an expensive and risky global arms race. (Of course, if the Soviet rulers had been smarter, they could have resisted joining that competition on Washington's terms, as China's Communist rulers have since the 1970s.) But if the Western countries had not also used the "constructive engagement" approach of Helsinki, the Soviet Empire could never have been dismantled in such a far-reaching and peaceable way.

In South Africa, as noted above, our government's combination of sanctions with diplomatic engagement was similarly successful. There are many other countries, too, in which diplomatic engagement has led to significant improvements in human rights. Where this approach has worked well, it has been one that treated everyone involved with respect, sought to understand and respond to the concerns of all parties, and did not heap public shame on any government leader, however heinous his acts may have been. Where it has not worked well has been when a U.S. secretary of state has publicly delivered hectoring, "nanny knows best" lectures to leaders in other countries, as Secretary of State Condoleezza Rice has done on numerous occasions.

Other Pointers for an Action Agenda on Rights

1. We need to recognize the importance of social and economic rights, not just civil and political rights.

As noted in Box 4.2, U.S. rights activists have generally placed more emphasis on the civil and political rights of people in other countries, saying relatively little about the economic and social rights agenda. However, most people in low-income countries argue that both kinds of rights need to go together. They note correctly that it is hard to exercise full civil and political rights if you or your family are hungry, if you do not have a sustainable livelihood, or if you have no access to a decent education, a basic transportation system, or a telephone. Many of us well understand how, within the United States, barriers like these to full social and economic inclusion can also keep low-income people underrepresented in political decision-making. The same is even more true in the global community.

The Indian-British philosopher Amartya Sen has meanwhile argued that respect for civil and political rights is necessary if people's access to social and economic rights is to be ensured. What we need, then, is for our government to take the whole spectrum of human rights seriously. It should start by—finally!—ratifying the International Covenant on Economic and Social Rights. (Our government's adherence to that important document would help a lot of low-income Americans, too.)

2. Understanding the link between conflict and atrocities.

Back in the 1970s, when the modern human rights movement became established, most of the abuses its activists documented were those committed by excessively strong, dictatorial governments in Eastern Europe or Latin America. These days, most of the worst abuses being committed around the world occur in countries where, very often, *the state is weak or functionally nonexistent,* a large proportion of the population has suffered from a collapse of livelihoods, and there have been massive migrations of destitute humanity across or within national borders. In such circumstances, intergroup conflicts frequently do not just erupt but become persistent; and those conflicts then become powerful incubators of atrocities. This has been the situation in numerous countries in sub-Saharan Africa as well as in Myanmar (Burma)—and of course, in Iraq.

Within the United States, we can respond to a single sociopath like the Unabomber or Timothy McVeigh with the full weight of our criminal justice system. But in countries racked by large-scale armed conflict, using the criminal justice system to contain or incapacitate perpetrators of gross violence is usually not possible. Often, the state's institutions have collapsed completely. Or the people who commit the atrocities are well connected to powerful political factions that refuse to act against them. In nearly all those places, too, atrocities are committed by numerous "sides" in the conflict, not just one. That helps keep the cycle of violence going. It also makes it hard to assemble the prorights coalition needed to stop the atrocities.

Many in the human rights movement think that an International Criminal Court (ICC) can solve this problem. But whether we have an effective ICC or not, we still need our government and the United Nations to keep their primary focus on helping all the parties to these harmful conflicts to *get them resolved,* since resolving the conflicts is the best guarantee for preventing future atrocities, and for reinstating the strong norms against killing that exist in all settled and peaceful societies. As noted earlier, resolving these kinds of conflicts involves paying close attention to all the dimensions of the human security agenda, including finding politically inclusive ways to end the intergroup conflicts that lie at their heart. Meanwhile, whenever there is an escalation of armed combat—undertaken by the United States or any other party—we can predict confidently that the rights of the residents of the war zone will be the main casualties.

3. Rights respect begins at home.

Many U.S. citizens want to see our government play a big role in the global rights movement. We need to recognize, though, that right now Washington has almost zero credibility when it speaks about human rights issues in other countries. In recent years, when I have spoken to non-Americans about the U.S. position on human rights, they answer by saying simply, "Abu Ghraib," or "Guantánamo."

So yes, it would be good if we could see the U.S. government playing an effective role in human rights questions around the world. But to push for this, global includers need to play close attention to our government's own record. Action on ensuring basic human rights worldwide must absolutely begin at home.

5

Climate Change

In wealthy countries, the looming climate crisis is a matter of concern.... In Africa, however, a region that has hardly contributed to climate change—its greenhouse gas emissions are negligible when compared with the industrialized world's—it will be a matter of life and death.

—Wangari Maathai, Nobel Peace Laureate, 2004

The evidence of the existence and extent of human-caused change to our planet's climate has become stronger and of greater concern than ever. In spring 2007, the scientists of the UN-based Intergovernmental Panel on Climate Change reported that they now had "very high confidence" that the net global effect of human activities since 1750 has been one of warming. They noted that their best forecasting models showed that temperatures over most land masses were "virtually certain" to increase over the twenty-first century, and heavy precipitation events were "very likely" to become more frequent.[1]

Indeed, the panel's scientists—and the rest of us—now have increasingly solid evidence that those effects, along with the shrinking of the polar ice caps and an associated rise in sea levels, are already under way. In recent years large-scale storms have become more frequent, more intense, and often much more damaging—on our own continent and in many other parts of the world.

Climate change affects all of humanity. For us as Americans it provides a crucial litmus test of what we want our country's relationship with the rest of the world to be. Do we want our country to be included as a responsible and constructive part of the world community—or do we want our government to pursue only a unilateral form of "national interest" advocated by a small number of large, carbon-guzzling corporations? This is a momentous choice. In fifty years our grandchildren will be living with the results of the choices we make today.

Global includers should keep in mind some key facts about our country's relationship to global warming:

1. Until very recently, the United States was the single heaviest emitter of the key greenhouse gas, carbon dioxide.

Environmental scientists have identified six key gaseous by-products of industrial processes the emission of which into the atmosphere contributes significantly to global warming. Of these, CFCs, which ripped apart the ozone layer, have already been brought under control through coordinated international action. By far the most significant of the other greenhouse gases is carbon dioxide (CO_2), a very common by-product of power plants, industrial processes, motor vehicles, and large-scale mechanized agriculture.

Figure 5.1 shows U.S. government figures for the CO_2 emissions of various countries, regions, and the world in 2004.

The solid bars show each country's or bloc's total emissions, and the diamond points joined by a line show their *per head* CO_2 emissions—both, according to the scale indicated in the legend. From the per-head data, note that Europe and Japan both have been able to sustain the strong economic records mentioned in earlier chapters even as they brought their CO_2 emissions down to *less than half the per-head rate* of the United States.

Sometime in 2007, China likely pulled a little ahead of the United States in terms of *total* CO_2 emissions. But of the world's significant economies, the United States was still by far the highest per-head emitter of CO_2. (Indeed, it has held that record for many decades now.)

2. **The United States is now the only significant country not involved in the international "Kyoto" process for reducing greenhouse gas emissions.**

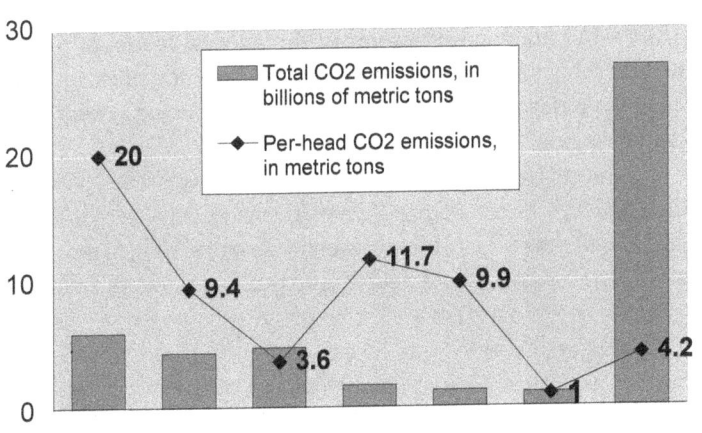

Figure 5.1 CO_2 Emissions, by Some Countries and Groupings, 2004[2]

In the Clinton era, U.S. diplomats helped negotiate the UN-sponsored Kyoto Protocol. But Clinton never even sent the treaty to the Senate for ratification. Then, when George W. Bush became president, he announced his firm opposition to it. On environmental policy, as in many other fields of action, Bush was adamant the United States should proceed unilaterally rather than committing itself to observance of limits negotiated with other countries.

By the end of 2007, 174 governments had ratified Kyoto. In doing so, the EU countries, Canada, Japan, and the treaty's other high-income signers all undertook by 2012 to reduce their emissions of CO_2 and the five other greenhouse gases to *5.2 percent below their 1990 levels.* (The treaty does not go beyond 2012.) For most of those countries, that effort involves a reduction of more than 20 percent below their emission level in 2000. The less-developed countries that signed Kyoto were held to no such reductions or limits, but they could benefit from its Clean Development Mechanism (CDM), which helps them become significantly "greener" as they grow their nations' economies. The biggest beneficiaries of CDM credits have been China, India, and Brazil, which have used them to close inefficient factories and power plants and undertake big reforestation projects.

The Kyoto Protocol is a far from perfect agreement. But it would have been a lot more effective if the United States had participated.

3. In the absence of strong environmental leadership from the federal government, many U.S. states, groups of states, and cities have developed their own plans for reducing greenhouse gas emissions.

One recent leader in this effort was California, where in 2006 Governor Arnold Schwarzenegger signed a bill mandating that by 2020 the state cut its emissions of the six greenhouse gases back to their 1990 levels. Schwarzenegger was building on a strong legacy of state-level progreen activism in California. One other early leader in legislating state-level green policies was Texas, under then-governor George W. Bush! In 1999, Bush helped push through legislation that required Texas electricity providers to increase their production of renewable energy by 2,000 megawatts within ten years. With that boost, Texas became a nationwide leader in wind-power generation and later adopted even more ambitious goals on renewables. As of 2007, twenty-one states and the District of Columbia had adopted renewable energy standards.[3]

These subfederal efforts have been important both because of their effect in helping to curb harmful emissions and because their adoption has shown the breadth of Americans' commitment to reducing global warming. However, no amount of subfederal action in environmental policy can substitute for committed nationwide action. (We can note, too, that even California's much-lauded targets were far less ambitious than those required by Kyoto.)

4. The foreseeable burdens of global warming are falling disproportionately on the poorest countries and communities around the world.

We could think of the whole world today as analogous to the state of Louisiana on the eve of Hurricane Katrina. Better-off families tend to live on higher ground; they have homes with stronger foundations, and more possibilities for escape. The lower-income families are concentrated on the lower ground, in more vulnerable structures, and have far fewer ways to get out. Then, the storm intensifies and the waters start to rise . . .

How will we in the United States respond as large-scale, warming-related disasters continue to multiply around the world?

Echoing the statement from Wangari Maathai at the beginning of this chapter, the experienced aid group Oxfam tells us:

> There is a deep injustice in the impacts of climate change. Rich countries have caused the problem with many decades of greenhouse-gas emissions (and in the process have grown richer). But poor countries will be worst affected, facing greater droughts, floods, hunger, and disease. . . .
>
> [G]iven their historic role in causing the problem, rich countries now have two extraordinarily clear obligations: to *stop harming,* by massively cutting their greenhouse-gas emissions, and to *start helping,* by providing compensatory finance so that poor countries can adapt, before they suffer the full impacts of climate change.[4]

By some estimates, the number of people who will be displaced by the rising sea levels from low-lying areas in Bangladesh, China, and Africa could rise into the hundreds of millions by 2050—or perhaps sooner. Desertification of large parts of Africa has already displaced entire communities and sent waves of desperate migrants to other, already stressed parts of Africa, and even on rickety boats across lethal seas to Europe and the Arabian Peninsula. Extreme degradation of once fertile environments and the resulting competition for scarce resources have contributed heavily to atrocity-laden conflicts in Darfur and elsewhere.

Even the U.S. Army War College has paid attention. War College professor Douglas V. Johnson II recently wrote: "The broader impact of serious climate change will require *multinational, multiagency cooperation on a scale heretofore unimaginable.* ... Should global cooperative measures fail, the first impact will likely come from large numbers of displaced people who, by the very nature of their displacement, will become subject to malnutrition and disease ... and border security issues could arise as well."[5]

Planning for the Future

Most U.S. allies have been considerably more forward-leaning than Washington in recognizing the need for worldwide cooperation in meeting the challenge of climate change. As noted above, all of the advanced industrial countries except the United States have been part of the Kyoto process. Germany, pushed by its influential Green Party, has shown a particularly strong commitment to reducing greenhouse gas emissions. Between 1988 and 2003, it reduced its per-head emissions of CO_2 by 20 percent (but still increased its per-head GDP by more than 30 percent.) We can learn a lot from Germany's example!

In the United Kingdom in 2006, the government's lead economist, Nicholas Stern, did an in-depth analysis of the best science available on warming, and of the economics of the worldwide effort required to bring it under control. He concluded that to cap global warming at anything like an acceptable level, the entire world's annual emission of CO_2 needs to be brought *beneath 5 billion metric tons*—that is, to around five-sixths of the level currently emitted by just the United States alone! (Stern judged that at that level, healthy forests worldwide could reabsorb each year's emissions, and there would be little additional warming.) Obviously, the sooner emissions can be reduced to that level, the less overall harm will have been inflicted on the geosphere in the meantime.

Stern warned that the costs of (1) restructuring economic systems that have until now been highly dependent on carbon fuels, and (2) supporting adaptation to climate change, especially in low-income countries, would be "significant, but manageable." He argued, "Above all, reducing the risks of climate change requires collective action. *It requires cooperation between countries, through international frameworks that support the achievement of shared goals.* ... Delay would be costly and dangerous."[6]

For us as Americans, Stern's conclusions present a particular challenge. Many of us have come to some understanding that the carbon-dependent way our economy has been structured until now has been harmful to the earth and that it continues, through its disproportionate puffing out of CO_2 into the atmosphere, to inflict additional harm on everyone around the world (including ourselves.) But what can we do about it?

We need to take decisive action at all levels: in our personal habits, in our communities and states, and also at the national and international levels.

Internationally, the fact that the Kyoto agreement in effect expires in 2012 gives our country a crucial opportunity to rejoin the worldwide effort to reduce greenhouse gas emissions on terms that are reasonable, effective, and manageable. The years between 2008 and 2012 will be vital in this regard. In one important sense, the United States never left the international climate control effort. Kyoto is not, technically, a treaty in its own right, but a protocol subsidiary to a broader 1992 treaty called the UN Framework Convention on Climate Change (UNFCCC). Although the United States never ratified Kyoto, it has remained a member of the UNFCCC, and this body is convening the main negotiations over *what to do after 2012.*

That negotiation was launched at a conference in Bali in December 2007. The conference proved much more dramatic than most such gatherings! The negotiations were so tough that the organizers had to schedule an extra day. As it drew toward its end, Paula Dobriansky, who headed the U.S. delegation, was openly booed when she said the United States could not join a binding Kyoto-style follow-up agreement; she was then publicly scolded by the next speaker, who came from tiny Papua New Guinea. Minutes after those humiliating moments Dobriansky reversed herself, announcing that the United States would, after all, be taking part in the negotiations on a binding agreement. The other conferees, relieved but exhausted, finally gave her a round of applause.

To contribute constructively to the remaining two years of the post-Bali negotiation, Americans need to be realistic on a number of key points:

- We should recognize, and be prepared to acknowledge to others, that the carbon-dependent way our country's economy was for so long structured—like those of all other high-income countries—has unintentionally inflicted (and to this day inflicts) real harms on the world's climate and well-being.
- We should understand that the vast majority of the world's people want and need us to deal with them fairly in this matter. In my travels around the world, many people—even individuals who admire our country a lot—have told me they were mystified why the United States stayed out of Kyoto and why so many Americans still seem so addicted to overlarge, gas-guzzling cars. Many asked, too, whether the "real" reason for the U.S. invasion of Iraq was a desire to control the world's oil pumps, to keep feeding our gasoline dependency. In today's global political "climate," the rest of the world's people do not see Americans as so special or virtuous that they need to cut us any further slack on global warming.
- We need to show a lot of realism—and a sense of international fairness—by being ready to commit ourselves to the kinds of deep technological change required to reduce our carbon emissions drastically. As the Oxfam report put it, we need to *stop harming* the whole of humanity and the bounteous earth that has sustained us all until now.

Some opponents of the Kyoto process have argued that technical innovation will, on its own, be sufficient to rescue our economy from its current deep carbon dependency. But as the experiences in Texas, Germany, and elsewhere have shown, it is only within a regulatory context established by committed political leadership that the necessary degree of progreen innovation can be incubated successfully. This is just as true at the U.S. national level and internationally as it is at the subfederal level.

Action at the National Level

An effective policy of global inclusion requires a federal government with a bold plan to cap and then reduce our country's carbon emissions. We U.S. citizens should demand that our leaders speedily produce and pursue a plan based on the following elements:

- *A firm, first-stage goal for reducing our country's total emissions*—for example, a reduction of 10 percent from the 2000 level by 2018. In an earlier era, President Kennedy established a clear target date for putting a man on the moon, and then galvanized the whole country into developing and funding the innovative technology required to meet it. Now, we need an equally bold but achievable national target for the even more important goal of reducing our country's carbon emissions.
- *The regulatory and financing mechanisms needed to achieve this goal.* Innovation on the required scale is not cheap, but there are many creative and politically sustainable ways to fund it. "Cap and trade" schemes and the establishment of a market in emission rights is one approach, but others may work equally well or perhaps better. Germany, California, and Texas all found ways to share the costs of innovation broadly—and without using a lot of tax revenue to do so.
- *An end to existing subsidies for high-emissions carbon fuels.* It is hard to believe, but Washington is still giving subsidies to the domestic oil and coal industries. Global includers would work to

end these subsidies (like the farm subsidies discussed in Chapter 3) quickly. This will provide a major spur to the development of renewables—and free up further funds to support that process.

- *Act at all stages and levels of the national economy.* Increasing the contribution of renewables to power generation and vehicle powering is only the start. (We need to be wary of some proposed solutions—see Box 5.1.) We also need to move rapidly toward low-carbon or no-carbon solutions in manufacturing and agriculture. We need to revise zoning approaches and habitation patterns that in most of the country foster a debilitating reliance on automobiles, and invest heavily in attractive, large-scale, no-carbon or low-carbon transit systems.
- *Accentuate the many side benefits of bringing emissions levels down.* Germany, Japan, and other countries have shown that emissions can be curbed considerably even as economic growth continues, not least because the spirit of innovation needed to reduce CO_2 emissions spreads rapidly across the whole economy. In reducing emissions, we will reduce energy costs along with our dependency on the world oil market. Smart, progreen planning supported by excellent transit systems can provide a better quality of life than widely spread suburbs linked only by clogged highways.
- *Upgrade the Environmental Protection Agency to administer this important national effort.* At present, the EPA is less than a full government department. It should be made into one, given a broad new mandate to push through the emissions-reduction policy, and have its capabilities rebuilt after they were systematically decreased through the Bush years. An experienced national leader—perhaps Nobel Laureate Al Gore—should be named the country's first secretary for environmental protection.

International Action

As Stern noted, effective international cooperation is crucial if global warming—the most truly "global" problem one can imagine—is to be

Box 5.1 Alternatives to Fossil Fuels

As the problems associated with fossil fuels have become more evident, people have been searching for less damaging alternatives. Many of these alternatives are now much more efficient and affordable than before. However, some raise their own further questions. Here is a quick guide:

Safe renewables: Wind power, wave power, geothermal (that is, the power of geysers and other thermal features), solar photovoltaic, and small-scale hydropower are all widely used to generate electricity. Passive solar power can efficiently heat water for domestic or small commercial uses. Vegetable matter (biomass) or the methane from animal excreta or landfills (biogas) is used to heat water or power machines. The two latter fuels emit some CO_2, though emissions can be minimized.

Possibly questionable renewables: Large-scale dams can generate a lot of power without emissions, but they have environmental and human consequences that must also be weighed.

Biofuels: The U.S. government recently increased its subsidies for bioethanol, which is produced from feed corn and used as a gasoline substitute. The EU has an even larger program to subsidize the production of biodiesel from oilseeds. These programs—but especially the creation of bioethanol from corn—require high inputs of energy relative to the power of the fuels produced. They also remove a great deal of fertile land from food production. They have already contributed to hefty rises in the price of food staples, which have badly hurt low-income people around the world. Creating twenty-five gallons of ethanol requires enough corn to feed a person for a year! Biofuels from the more woody ("cellulosic") by-products of food production may be a better option, but the technology has not yet been effectively developed.

Nuclear: China is now undertaking a big expansion of its nuclear power capacity—from 10 gigawatt equivalents in mid-2007 to 160 GWe by 2030. Other countries, including the United States, are also planning to increase nuclear capacity. Nuclear power plants carry known risks from earthquakes. (The earthquake-prone Pacific Rim hosts all of China's plants as well as Japan's and South Korea's.) Nuclear plants and their fuels require extensive security measures. Production of nuclear fuels takes a lot of electricity, and disposing of them safely is a vast long-term challenge. Instead of pouring money into these plants, it probably would be wiser to invest the same amount into development of much safer renewables.

dealt with successfully. Our country needs to be a full and constructive part of that process.

Throughout most of George W. Bush's presidency, he steered clear of the diplomacy the world's other countries and the United Nations were conducting on environmental issues. In April 2001, Vice President Richard Cheney infamously told an audience in Canada that "[c]onservation may be a sign of personal virtue, but it is not a sufficient basis for a sound, comprehensive energy policy." (Cheney was in charge of the president's national task force on energy at the time.) By December 2007, however, the administration had been forced to change its stance on climate issues quite substantially, as Paula Dobriansky's dramatic Bali turnaround demonstrated. The post-Bali negotiations over how the world's countries will share the responsibilities of the antiwarming campaign after the Kyoto Protocol expires in 2012 are scheduled to be completed in December 2009.

Here are some guidelines for the priorities U.S. citizens should press our leaders to pursue as the negotiations continue:

1. Our country should be a full party to whatever international arrangement follows the expiration of Kyoto in 2012.

The arguments for joining the rest of the world in the new, post-2012 regime are even stronger than the earlier arguments were for joining Kyoto. Today, we know a lot more about the magnitude of the climate change challenge than we knew ten years ago. Also, technology experts, business leaders, and policy-makers around the world know a lot more now than they did then about the technologies and regulatory and financial mechanisms that can help the world's peoples meet this challenge.

There is now also a new, compelling reason for the United States to be part of the impending international arrangement. To be effective, any antiwarming effort will have to include China—and other rapidly developing countries—in the cap-and-reduce effort, and not just as beneficiaries of CDM credits. Figure 5.2 shows how China's total emissions were approaching ours in 2004. Since then they have probably overtaken those of the United States. If the United States, which still puts out an extremely high level of emissions for every citizen, does not join in good faith in an internationally negotiated effort to cap and reduce, then we should not have any illusions that we could persuade China or other emerging economies to do the same.

China's leaders have already started to work to increase the energy efficiency of the factories and generating plants that have powered their country's recent impressive surge of economic growth. They have also made large investments in renewable energy. But they remain understandably unwilling to give up on the goal of growth itself, arguing that their people have the right to enjoy the same levels of economic well-being that people in the already industrialized countries have.[7] One of the world's biggest challenges over the next dozen years will be to engage China's leaders and people in a new kind of global discussion over how the goals of the Chinese people and those of the rest of humanity all can be fairly and sustainably met. Americans need to be part of this discussion. But the entry price will be our own willingness to participate in good faith in a fair, worldwide process.

2. We need to help fund other countries' mitigation and adaptation measures as well as our own.

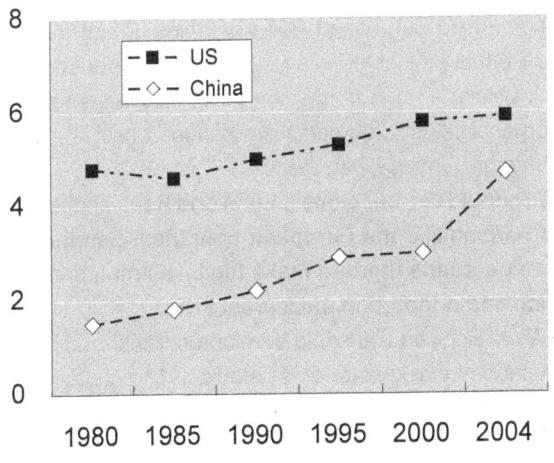

Figure 5.2 U.S. and China, Converging CO_2 Emissions, in Billions of Metric Tons[8]

The Stern review made clear that early investment in *mitigation* of global warming, by reducing nearly every country's CO_2 emissions, will save a considerable amount of the money needed to undertake even more drastic, and much more expensive, *adaptation* measures in future decades. (This is in line with the strong "Human Security" principle that investing in prevention is better than waiting and then having to pay for a more expensive cure later.) But we also need to start investing in adaptation measures, building the resilience of threatened communities both at home and abroad. For some communities, relocation may be the only answer, in which case it should be undertaken in an inclusive and fair way that strengthens communities and the families that constitute them. Other forms of adaptation will be needed, too, if the lives and livelihoods of those threatened by climate change are to be saved.

The international community already has one major financing mechanism, the Global Environmental Fund (GEF), that supports various environmental protection projects around the world. However, the funding for adaptation in low-income countries needs to be increased further. The Oxfam report cited above argues that funding for this purpose should be provided *in addition to* regular overseas aid. It also argues that responsibility for funding low-income countries' adaptation projects should be divided among the well-off countries according to a formula that looks at their ability to contribute and their responsibility for having caused CO_2-based global warming up until now. Oxfam's formula, like that advocated in a recent study supported by Christian Aid (UK), places a huge burden on the United States and the EU.[9] These organizations' arguments are serious ones, and Americans should engage seriously with them.

3. We should use our clout in the World Bank and IMF, and with well-off nations like the European countries, Saudi Arabia, and Japan, to persuade them to make big investments in worldwide mitigation and adaptation measures, too.

The World Bank and other big development financing bodies spent many decades funding large-scale road-building and power-generation projects that locked many low- and middle-income countries into heavily carbon-dependent development paths. It was only after the

1990 Earth Summit that the World Bank started to invest some funds in intentionally progreen projects. In 2006, it invested $860 million in renewable energy and energy efficiency projects. But that sum was only a tiny proportion of the $23.6 billion in loans to which the bank committed in 2006, and was far outweighed by the bank's continuing support for carbon-heavy energy projects. That needs to change.

Reconnecting with the World over Climate Change

For the rest of the twenty-first century, the single greatest challenge to human life and civilization will be the one posed by the deep-seated, human-induced change occurring in our planet's climate. No country in the world can afford to continue with the unthinking pumping out into the earth's atmosphere of carbon-based waste gases in the way that Americans, Europeans, and Japanese all did during our economic growth periods of the past 150 years. Today, all of humanity is threatened by the consequences of global warming. The costs of global warming know no national boundaries. All of humanity now needs to pull together to curb the warming and to find alternative, environmentally sustainable paths to economic well-being.

Until recently, some American politicians argued that our country could stand aside from the antiwarming efforts pursued by the rest of the world. Today—after all we have seen of catastrophic weather effects in recent years, and as we watch the emergence of the world's new first-rank carbon emitter, China—it is clear that unilateralism is not an answer. There is no way our country, or any country, can ever "control" its way out of this problem. We need to reinclude our country in the global antiwarming effort.

6

Global Power Shifts

This world of ours ... must avoid becoming a community of dreadful fear and hate, and be, instead, a proud confederation of mutual trust and respect.

—Dwight D. Eisenhower

Throughout most of George W. Bush's presidency, Bush himself and nearly all other U.S. politicians and opinion leaders were focusing their attention on Al-Qaeda terrorism and Iraq. Meanwhile, two other important developments in world politics went woefully undernoticed. The first was the mounting challenge of human-induced climate change. The second was a seismic shift in the balance of power among the world's nations. The German writer Josef Joffe has, as noted in Chapter 1, described the role the United States played in the world in the 1990s as that of the world's sole "überpower." That description was appropriate—then. But in the early years of the new century the situation started to change, and the pace of that change was certainly accelerated by the fallout from Bush's extremely ill-considered decision to invade Iraq.

By late 2007, our country's standing relative to that of other world powers had shifted a lot. One example: by June 2007, some $2.2 trillion of our $9 trillion of federal debt was held by foreigners, and of that, $405 billion was held by the People's Bank of China. Those treasury bill holdings made up less than one-third of China's total U.S. dollar holdings. At the end of September 2007 China's dollar holdings totaled $1.43 trillion, giving Beijing considerable power over the dollar—but at the same time, a huge stake in its strength. (One Chinese bank reportedly lost a lot of money in the U.S.-based subprime mortgage crisis of 2007.)

The economic growth China has achieved since 1980 has indeed been extraordinary. As Figure 6.1 indicates, by 2005 China's share of the world economy, as measured in "international" dollars that take into account the dollar's different purchasing power in each country, had risen to fairly close to the U.S. share—up from just a fraction of the U.S. share in 1980.

It is not just China that has been amassing economic power. The expansion of the European Union meant that by the turn of the millennium the EU economy had become greater than the U.S. economy. The Euro exchange rate against the dollar climbed nearly 50 percent between January 2003 and November 2007. India, which has a population almost as large as China's, has shown a significant economic takeoff. Japan, where hi-tech innovation is supported by Internet connections

Figure 6.1 U.S. and China's Changing Shares of World Economic Output (in "international" $), percent[1]

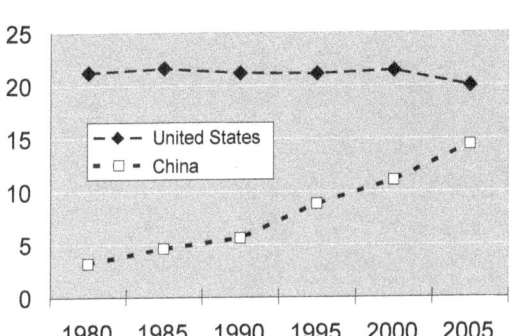

Note: An international $ is a measure that takes into account the different purchasing power of a dollar in each country.

on average twelve times as fast as ours, found ways to escape the economic sluggishness it showed in the 1990s. And by 2007 Russia's economy and society were showing new sturdiness, too.

At the purely economic level of national power, the performance of some nations and groups of nations as of 2005 was as shown in Figure 6.2.

Having a strong economy allows a country to exert its "muscle" in the international arena—whether by transforming some of its economic power into military power or by using economic instruments themselves to influence the decisions of other nations. But economic and military capabilities are not the only determinants of a nation's power. Other key determinants are the nation's human-resource base, including both the size and the skill set of its population, and cultural or reputational power, which has often been called "soft power" since Harvard professor Joseph S. Nye, Jr., developed that concept in 1990.

In today's hyperconnected world, soft power has become more important than ever. It can be thought of as including the following elements:

Figure 6.2 Economic Performance of Some Nations and Regions, 2005[2]

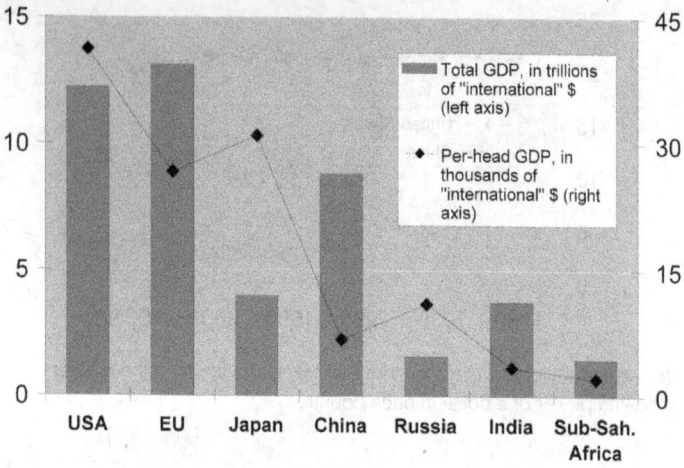

Note: An international $ is a measure that takes into account the different purchasing power of a dollar in each country.

1. the worldwide appeal of a country's ideals, culture, and institutions;
2. general global appreciation of its achievements;
3. the perceived truthfulness of its leaders on matters of global import; and
4. the country's reputation as a fair-minded upholder of the rules and norms of international society—also known as its international legitimacy.

Back in the 1990s, when the United States was still in the position of Joffe's überpower, it was number one in just about all the categories of national power. Militarily and economically we were clearly number one. Regarding human resources, our population was much smaller than that of China or India, but it was well educated. And regarding the various elements of soft power, our country was strongly admired in much—though not all—of the world. Our leaders were generally regarded as truthful on important matters. During the years of the Clinton administration, many non-Americans were perplexed that the United States did not join many of the newly emerging international treaties, but the United States nonetheless still had a strong reputation for upholding existing international rules and norms.

The actions of the Bush administration—in Iraq, in the "War on Terror," and elsewhere—have changed all that. The damage to our nation's standing was particularly great in the realm of soft power. Our country's ideals, and the sincerity with which our leaders proclaimed them, were derided worldwide in light of the U.S. interrogation policies in Abu Ghraib, Guantánamo, and Afghanistan and the hypocrisy Bush displayed in his on-again-off-again campaigns for worldwide democracy. Our reputation as a "can do" nation was badly dented by the incompetence Washington showed in its administration of post-invasion Iraq and its response to Hurricane Katrina. Most seriously of all, the U.S. reputation as a fair-minded upholder of established global norms—of international legitimacy—was shredded by Bush's decisions (1) to invade Iraq in the absence of any compelling *casus belli,* and (2) to show itself so ready to bend or break the Geneva Conventions.

By 2007 it had become clear that our country was no longer anywhere near number one in terms of soft power. Regarding economic power, the Bush years generated a notable decline in the U.S. share of world economic output, as indicated earlier. The federal government's budgets, which under Clinton had started to show some surplus, plunged back into deficit; and, as noted, a significant portion of the growing national debt that resulted was held by foreign governments. Regarding human resources, the generally well-educated population of the EU now, after the EU's expansion, exceeds ours by about 50 percent. And over recent years China and India have both been graduating engineers and scientists in numbers far greater than the United States.

The only area in which we have retained a clear number one slot was military might. But meanwhile, as the hard-to-end U.S. entanglement in Iraq showed—in today's hyperconnected world more than ever before—raw military power has become incapable, on its own, of achieving and hanging on to goals of real strategic significance. Today, all nations, *even the number one military nation,* need to have both diplomatic/political smarts and strong diplomatic alliances if they are to succeed in making and holding on to any worthwhile strategic gains. And the only way to win and keep allies in today's world is by keeping one's good reputation as a team player—as a rule-keeper rather than rule-breaker, and an upholder of international legitimacy.

So long as our country retained its role as the unchallenged sole world überpower—the undisputed winner of the Cold War, or the world's "indispensable nation," as Clinton described it—many powerful Americans felt it did not matter too much whether our country played by the international rules or not. Indeed, there was a fairly broad distrust of the whole idea of such rules, since many members of the U.S. political elite felt they might be applied in a way that would constrain U.S. use of its own power around the world.

A certain amount of that distrust was evident in the actions of the Clinton administration, but under George W. Bush it became a central pillar of his diplomacy. Back in 2000, Condoleezza Rice published an article that defined the broad principles she took with her when she became Bush's national security advisor in January 2001. She argued strongly that the United States should no longer feel obliged to comply with long-standing international agreements. And she treated with apparent disdain the idea that the United States might have any obligation to the rest of the world, writing: "To be sure, there is nothing wrong with doing something that benefits all humanity, but that is, in a sense, a second-order effect."[3] Then, as we have seen in earlier chapters, after Bush became president he quickly walked away from the Kyoto Protocol and a number of other key international agreements.

By 2008, however, it had become clear that the ideals of maintaining mutual respect and a spirit of fairness and reciprocity among the world's nations were just as important to everyone in the world—including Americans—as they ever had been. There were three main reasons for this:

1. The earlier assumption that many Americans had that Washington's primacy in world affairs could last for a long time—even, in the version favored by many Bush cabinet members, for a

whole "New American Century"—proved to be badly flawed. The whole world is now undergoing deep shifts in the balance of international power. Any such shift in the global balance of power can be unsettling and entail sizable risks of international misunderstanding, or worse. At such a time, adherence to (and reliance on) long-recognized rules and norms of behavior are all the more important.
2. Precisely because the United States is no longer an überpower that can easily dominate every area of international life, Americans now need to be able to work in an effective and predictable way with other nations. That requires "rules of international engagement." Non-überpower nations always understood this. We need to relearn it.
3. The world's fastest rising power, China, is a large and potentially extremely capable country that has so far played well by the basic rules of international behavior established—by the United States—in 1945, and also by the rules of the world trade system. (China has been a full member of the WTO since 2001.) As China continues to rise, it is in the strong interest of Americans, Chinese, and everyone else in the world that the existing rule system be reaffirmed and strengthened or reformed as necessary rather than weakened in any way.

The Importance of the United Nations

As we think seriously about the shifts under way in the world power balance, global includers should be more grateful than ever for the vision of Presidents Franklin D. Roosevelt and Harry Truman when they dealt with the even more abrupt shift in the global balance of power in 1945. At that point, our country suddenly found itself much more powerful on the global scene than it had ever been before. Much of Europe and Asia lay in rubble. The United States, with its cities untouched by physical attack and its factories and farms working overtime, had its massive military straddling the world's oceans. It had unparalleled power to dictate the terms of peace that would follow. Only Soviet Russia had some ability to check U.S. power, but given the destruction both Hitler and Stalin had visited on Russia over preceding years, that capability was limited.

Some prominent Americans argued in 1945 for harsh policies toward occupied Germany and Japan and other forms of strategic triumphalism. Others called for the United States to retreat into isolationism. Roosevelt and Truman resisted both impulses. They dismissed the idea of imposing tough collective punishments on Germany or Japan. They were determined, too, that the United States stay strongly involved in international affairs; and they established a visionary rule-based network of institutions for that purpose, with the United Nations at its core.

We all—Americans and non-Americans—are lucky that, as we face the challenges of the decades ahead, we do not start from a situation of unordered global chaos, but we have the strong foundation of the United Nations on which to build. It is true that the United Nations is far from perfect. Its internal decision-making processes need considerable reform. The idea that just five governments—including countries as small as France and the UK!—each have a veto on the Security Council is quite an unsustainable remnant of the old control paradigm.

Another problem with the UN decision-making rules is that each of the world's recognized national governments gets one, and just one, seat in the General Assembly. This means that Seychelles, population 86,000, has formal equality with China, population 1.3 billion. It also means that all those peoples around the world who do not have states of their own—the Kurds, Tibetans, Xoisan, Navajo, Darfuris, and so on—have no voice in the United Nations. One good way to address both problems would be to create a global "lower house" of decision-making for the United Nations, with a more truly proportional form of representation. This body could act as a broader check on the UN General Assembly and Security Council.

The United Nations has undergone significant internal reforms since the end of the Cold War, which significantly increased both its efficiency and its effectiveness. But its internal administration is still less transparent and accountable than it should be—though it harbors far less waste, fraud, and abuse than its critics in the United States claim (and less, too, than some of the more poorly regulated arms of the U.S. government). But still, with good will and forethought all around, the United Nations is reformable. Meanwhile, having it in existence at the present turning point in world affairs is still certainly a lot better than *not* having it.

A Collaborative U.S. Role in the World?

In 2006, the Chicago Council on Global Affairs (CCGA) contracted with respected polling organizations in the United States and fourteen other countries to survey the opinions of those countries' citizens about the U.S. role in the world. Respondents were asked to identify their preferred view of the U.S. role from among the following options:

A. "As the sole remaining superpower, the United States should continue to be the preeminent world leader in solving international problems."
B. "The United States should do its share in efforts to solve international problems together with other countries."
C. "The United States should withdraw from most efforts to solve international problems."

Their responses were as charted in Figure 6.3, which echo the results of other similar surveys in recent years. The answers tell us some significant things:

- U.S. respondents did *not* seek a "preeminent" role for Washington in solving world problems, regardless of the rhetoric or assumptions of most U.S. politicians. A strong majority (75 percent) of Americans *favored U.S. participation in a shared leadership system.*
- Only in India and Israel did more than 20 percent of respondents favor a preeminent U.S. role. Everywhere else, it was under 20 percent.
- Of the fifteen countries polled, *all except four showed a strong preference for the shared leadership model.* The standouts were Argentina and the Palestinian territories, where the citizens

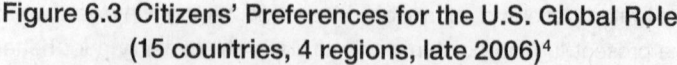

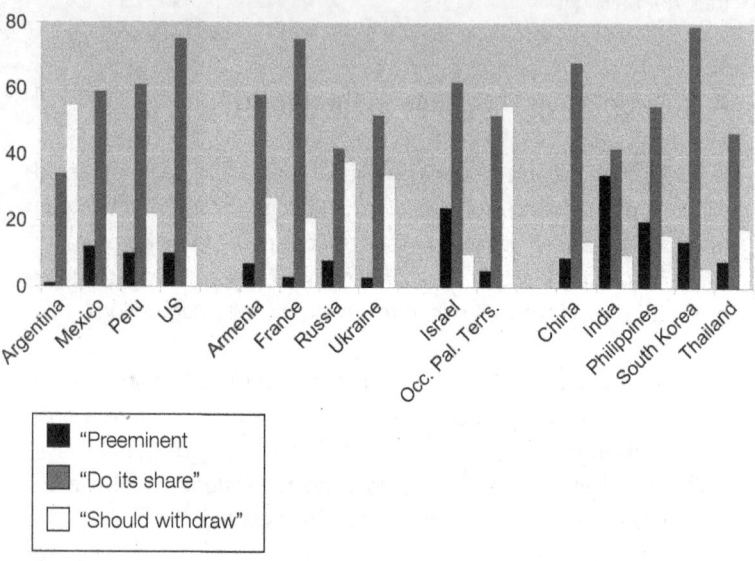

favored complete U.S. withdrawal from leadership; and India and Russia, where there was a preference for shared leadership over the other options, but only a small one.
- In the other eleven countries polled, *including the United States,* the preference for shared leadership was strong indeed.

Another significant finding from that poll was that 76 percent of Americans thought our country was playing the role of world police force more than it should.

The CCGA warned that this poll was not wholly representative of national opinions. In addition to the usual uncertainties involved in polling, in some of these countries the samples were restricted to urban areas. (Keep in mind, too, that the populations of the nations polled vary widely. For example, China and India have more than 1 billion citizens each, and Armenia has just 3 million.) Nevertheless, this poll and others like it can give helpful indications of sentiments around the world.

One of the most perceptive analysts of the U.S. role in the world is Kishore Mahbubani, who was Singapore's ambassador to the United Nations in 2001–2002. (He chaired the UN Security Council in May 2002.) In a book published in 2005, Mahbubani described a world that had become more globalized than ever before. But he warned that the "global village" was marked by very stark economic inequalities and was *not* a happy place.

He recalled that in earlier eras, when European countries underwent rapid industrialization and the deep social change that accompanied it, their rulers staved off revolt and built a sense of national community by giving the poor the right to vote and creating social safety nets. But in today's global village,

> we are doing virtually the exact opposite.... Instead of enfranchising the poor of our planet, we are disenfranchising them. Almost all the key decisions that affect their lives are made without their having any vote or say. Nor are there any social safety nets. There are minuscule aid flows from the rich to the poor, but they are driven by political considerations, not humanitarian or long-term considerations.
>
> More importantly, there is no sense of community in this global village.... *[M]ost of the decisions that affect the fate of the whole village are made by one incredibly rich and powerful household, the American mansion.* Some of these decisions benefit the whole village. Many don't. The American household is blithely ignorant of the consequences of its actions for the rest of the village.[5]

In September 2005 I heard Mahbubani speak to an audience in Geneva about the choices the world—including the United States—faces in the present era. An unabashed admirer of the "American ideal," he recalled that in 1945 the United States had established the rule-based global system we know today. Over the decades that followed 1945, he said, the system provided a broadly (though not wholly) peaceful world environment and brought the benefits of economic development to an unprecedented number of the world's people. He noted that back in 1945 Presidents Roosevelt and Truman had simply assumed the system they were establishing would continue to operate under U.S. leadership. But he said that assumption was now open to serious questioning—primarily because of the lack of commitment recent U.S. governments have displayed to the ideals of international rules and global fairness.

In his book, Mahbubani wrote that there seemed to be a nearly irreconcilable clash between the self-referential attitudes and preferences of U.S. voters and the interests of the rest of the world's people. However, the information from the CCGA poll indicates strongly that this need not be the case. The U.S. respondents to that poll showed an apparently sophisticated understanding of the depth of our people's interdependence with the (much larger) non-U.S. portion of global humanity.

In August 2007, an organization called WorldPublicOpinion.org compiled the findings of numerous polls conducted on U.S. attitudes to global engagement in recent years. It found some similarly encouraging results:

- A "very strong majority" rejected the idea that the United States should take a more isolationist stance.
- A large majority was opposed to the way it perceived the United States was playing the role of dominant world leader: "Americans express surprisingly modest concern for preserving the U.S. role as the sole superpower."
- Very strong majorities favored the United States working through international institutions (especially the United Nations) and making international institutions more powerful.
- Americans "are reluctant to use military force except as part of multilateral efforts."
- A large majority favored the United States using multilateral approaches for dealing with terrorism, addressing international environmental issues, and giving aid for economic development.
- A large majority felt that U.S. foreign policy should at times serve altruistic purposes independent of U.S. national interests.
- Asked to set their own preferred levels for foreign aid, most Americans usually set them higher than the actual levels.[6]

Dealing with Global Power Shifts

So how should Americans deal with being a former überpower?

First, there is no cause for alarm. I grew up in a Britain that, at the time, seemed to be losing its power in the world rapidly. Every month, it seemed, an additional nation in Africa or Asia was gaining its independence from the bonds of empire. But as I noted in Chapter 1, withdrawing from the former empire turned out to be good for Britain—as it was for all of the other European powers that decolonized in those years. Being a former überpower will probably be just as good for Americans. It will enable us to deal in a far more friendly and constructive fashion with the rest of the world's peoples than we can ever hope to do if we try to retain strong U.S. "control" over everything that happens in the world.

Yes, perhaps we have some special concerns about the remarkable rise of China (see Box 6.1). It is clearly significant that China's central bank holds a sizable portion of our national debt. But at the economic level, our two peoples are already deeply interdependent. So it is not in Beijing's interest to do anything that would harm the U.S. economy drastically—and the reverse is true as well. Any escalation toward a trade war or other form of hostile confrontation would harm us all.

It's true, too, that many Americans (including me) have strong concerns about human rights abuses attributable to China's government—both those they commit at home and those committed by some of their allies overseas. But then, many people around the world (and in the United States) have strong concerns about the rights records of our government and some of its allies, too. How should we deal with these concerns? The best way is probably to discuss all of them in ways that are forward-looking, aimed at improving the situation of the people involved, and based on existing fair-minded human rights standards.

It probably would be helpful, too, if more Americans would voice acknowledgement of the real improvements in social and economic rights China's Communist rulers have helped their citizens secure in recent decades. For example, on the UN Human Development Index—a score that combines, on a single scale of zero to one, measures of per-head GDP with those for life expectancy, illiteracy, and school enrollment—China went up from 0.53 in 1975 to 0.77 in 2004. That represents a notable increase in human well-being for 1.3 billion Chinese citizens.

And certainly, many Americans, like many Chinese, have strong concerns about China's contribution to global warming and the prospect that continuation of China's current economic path might make this problem a lot worse over the decades ahead. As indicated in Chapter 5, *engaging* China in effective efforts to control greenhouse gas emissions is key to any attempt to curb global warming in the current century—but we have to be prepared to make solid commitments of our own in that regard, too.

So Americans have a lot to discuss with China. We have a lot to discuss with other nations, too, in the current era of transition from a one-überpower world to one in which power is more widely and, let us hope, more equitably distributed. These discussions should be broad and respectful, and should engage the citizens of the countries concerned as well as their governments. But at least today's generation of global includers have those visionary declarations and institutions that were crafted in 1945 by an earlier generation of U.S. leaders as a strong, agreed-upon foundation upon which to build.

Box 6.1 China Today

In the spring of 2004, I went to China with a small delegation of scholars. We had dozens of excellent conversations with professors and university administrators in Beijing and Shanghai. Many of these people had been teenagers during Mao Zedong's "Cultural Revolution" in the 1960s. One man told us how, as a young teen, he had taken part in the harsh public shaming of his teacher Mao called for in those days—and how, three decades later, he went back, found the teacher, and apologized to her. By then this man was a professor of education, working hard to rebuild China's educational system from the chaos into which the Cultural Revolution had thrown it. (By the way, he said his former teacher forgave him.)

China has come a long way since the Cultural Revolution. Today, Shanghai is an ultramodern city with elevated highways stacked four and five levels high that snake through new forests of high-design, high-rise buildings. In 2004 vast areas of Beijing became construction sites as the city prepared for the 2008 Olympics—we saw large-scale building projects in the other three cities we visited as well. Boxy retail malls offered luxurious Western brand names to China's newly rich entrepreneurs, and the many traditional street markets hummed with activity.

Some officials in the ruling Communist Party told us frankly of their concern that China's wealth should be spread more equitably among its people. Their concern was probably justified. After decades of Maoist-style egalitarianism, China has become openly consumerist. UN figures show that incomes there are now distributed about as unequally as those in the United States—but at lower income levels all around.

China, like India, now has a huge upper-middle class: its members love to travel inside and outside their country and have increasing opportunities to interact with foreigners. Most of the people we talked with expressed a strong preference for gradual political evolution, both domestically and in international affairs, over any further bouts of violent or "revolutionary" change.

7

Rejoining the Rest of the World

A spirit of harmony can only survive if each of us remembers, when bitterness and self-interest seem to prevail, that we share a common destiny.

—U.S. Rep. Barbara Jordan

Our Relationship with the Other 95 Percent of Humanity

In Chapter 1, I outlined a new way of thinking about our country's relationship with the world based on an idea of global inclusion, which highlights the need for Americans to build a new, more fair-minded relationship with the 95 percent of the world's people who are not U.S. citizens. I argued that a foreign policy based on global inclusion and the ideas of the human security movement can serve our real needs as Americans more reliably and sustainably than the control paradigm our government has followed until now.

Sitting here in our beautiful country, fundamentally secure behind its broad guardian oceans, with friendly powers to our south and north, it has been temptingly easy for Americans to ignore events in the rest of the world. But now, faced with the mounting challenge of global warming—which knows no earth-based boundaries at all—the interdependence between U.S. citizens and the world's 6 billion other people has become quite evident. For our own well-being, Americans today need to rely on the world's non-Americans *not* to follow the same high-emissions path we have followed up until now. And meanwhile, they are certainly counting on us to change our ways regarding our casual reliance on a high-emissions economic model. The well-being (and perhaps even survival) of U.S. citizens is in the hands of non-Americans, just as their well-being and perhaps survival are in ours.

The idea that all the world's peoples are deeply interdependent on each other lies at the heart of the theory of human security. Back in the 1990s, when this approach was first being explored and applied by countries like Canada and Norway, most Americans still ignored it, judging that our country's dominance in world affairs meant that any suggestion that the United States was interdependent with other countries could easily be dismissed.

However, as Bush's term in the White House draws toward its end, the counterproductive consequences of that unilateralist mind-set have become increasingly evident. It has become clearer than ever before that, yes, our country does still need to engage in active (and usually negotiated) cooperation with other countries *if our own security needs are to be met.* And if we need to rely on negotiations with other countries, that means we need to treat them as equals and on the basis of agreed-upon ground rules that are fair to everyone concerned. We cannot just ignore their concerns, but need to pay as much heed to them as we ask them to pay to ours.

We need to acknowledge frankly that, yes, we Americans are part of the web of interdependence that today ties all of humanity together. Yes, only through relying on the help of others can we resolve the precarious strategic/political situation an arrogant and ill-informed Washington helped to create in Iraq, Afghanistan, and elsewhere. Yes, relying on our connections with other countries is essential if we want to navigate a safe path through the large-scale power shifts the world is now undergoing. And yes, relying on and strengthening this web of international relationships is the only way we and the rest of humanity can find a way to meet the challenge of climate change.

The human security approach to strategic affairs is more relevant to our country's needs than ever before. We U.S. citizens and our leaders need to make the simple but profound mind-set shift of seeing ourselves as truly—and equally—a part of global humanity, rather than as somehow standing aside from (or above?) the rest of the world's peoples.

If we adopt the global inclusion approach to foreign policy, this can encourage us to start imagining what our role might be in a world marked more by cooperation, mutual respect, and reciprocity among peoples than by divisiveness and fear. And in line with the human security precept that true security is *people-centered rather than state-centered,* we can start thinking about our country's national interest in a new, more people-centered way, different from the "big power" way it has generally been understood until now.

We can start to identify the foundations of a citizen-centered definition of U.S. national interests by asking questions like these:

- Why would we simply assume it is in our interest as U.S. citizens that our government put so much funding into the military and so little into maintaining nonviolent ways of resolving or radically de-escalating our disagreements with other nations—and so little, too, into providing fair-minded, "untied" development aid to those in need?

- When did the other peoples of the world ever vote for the U.S. military to be the preeminent military force on distant land masses and in distant sea lanes, and why should we U.S. citizens continue to pay in blood and treasure to maintain that situation? What alternative, more collaborative, politically legitimate, and politically sustainable security arrangements might be more effective for the peoples of regions such as Africa, Asia, or the Persian Gulf (and for our relationship with those peoples)?
- Why would we imagine it is in the interest of U.S. citizens that our government continually bend the rules of international interaction in our people's favor, whether in military, diplomatic, or economic affairs, when past attempts to do this have so frequently ended up increasing anti-U.S. resentment around the world and making Americans *less* rather than more secure?
- What benefits do U.S. citizens gain when Washington hands special favors to big corporations in the agribusiness, automobile, mining, or other economic sectors that *inflict known and serious harms on people in other countries* and ruin our country's ability to be perceived as fair by the 6 billion other people in the world? (We should remember that these favors often harm other, less politically well-connected portions of our own economy and society, too.)
- Wouldn't a diplomacy based on a "golden rule" of treating the peoples of other countries with the same fairness, respect, and generosity that we hope to enjoy from them do more to build the real security of U.S. citizens than one that seeks to grab unilateral advantage for American corporations wherever it can?
- Why does our country's approach to the other peoples and governments of the world need to be marked so deeply by fearfulness and distrust, rather than by hope and a sense of possibility in what 6.3 billion people can achieve on this planet, if we all pull together? Why can't we reconnect with the friendship and egalitarianism so many Americans showed toward the rest of the world in the past, and so many non-Americans

have shown toward us throughout most of our history as a nation?
- Why do we need to be fearful of international institutions and norms that—in line with the values of an earlier generation of U.S. leaders—proclaim and work toward the goals of international fairness, global equality, and the avoidance of war?
- Why would we imagine it desirable that Washington and a few rich allies continue to hang on tightly to the reins of power in the institutions of global economic and political governance?

The poll data described in Chapter 6 show us that, in fact, many Americans have already been thinking realistically about these matters. The fact that in 2006, 75 percent of Americans expressed a preference for a shared leadership model of global governance rather than either continued U.S. preeminence or U.S. isolation is an incredible source of hope for global includers. (If you go to the WorldPublicOpinion.org website, you can find numerous other details about the sophistication of the American people's understanding of world affairs, too.)

A large body of Americans is savvy, too, in understanding the strong interconnections among the topics addressed in this book. People can see that building relationships of respect, equality, and generosity with other people around the world is a much better and more sustainable way to build our country's security than a continued quest for military domination, and that these principles of fairness and generosity should mark all the different strands of our dealings with others: in economics and trade, human rights, security affairs, and the environment.

We also need to start looking much more coolly and objectively at the effects our past and present actions have had on others and—in line with Oxfam's good advice on global warming—work to correct our country's actions so that we *stop harming* other people around the world, even as we try to *start helping* them. This advice is good in all areas of our interactions with others: in trade and military matters, and, of course, our government's human rights practices, as much as in the area of climate change.

Large numbers of Americans have been telling the pollsters, too, that they strongly appreciate the work of the United Nations. We are indeed lucky today that we have so many equality-based and intentionally nonmilitarist international institutions, rules, and norms on which to build. The UN Charter, the whole of the now well-developed body of human rights law, and even the WTO are all built on fundamentally egalitarian principles. Those principles may often have been imperfectly expressed in practice. But they give global includers a good jumping-off point from which to reform the policies both of Washington and of these institutions themselves.

Here is a conundrum, though. If so many members of the U.S. public are indeed so savvy in understanding the facts about our interdependence with the rest of the world, why is our country's decision-making still so heavily dominated by people who cling to the jingoistic rhetoric of the old control paradigm? Where are the disconnects?

I think there are disconnects at three levels: vision, self-confidence, and action.

At the level of vision, I know there are many Americans who feel, or know in some way, that the path our country has been following until now—in Iraq, on the environment, on the Geneva Conventions, and other issues—has been neither successful in meeting our people's real interests nor morally sound. But so far, we have not really had a unified and compelling vision of the kind of foreign policy we want to pursue instead and the values we want our country to uphold in the world. Global inclusion can provide such a vision.

Regarding self-confidence, it seemed to me that right after 9/11 large portions of the U.S. public were deeply traumatized by the tragic events of that day, and lacked the confidence in their own judgment to be able to stand up to the drumbeat of militarism from our leaders and much of the media that was telling us that a hard-hitting military response—"shock and awe!"—was the best way forward. For three or four years after 9/11, the effects of that traumatization lived on, stoked by the efforts of many leading figures in politics and the media to keep public fearfulness at a high level. As our leaders rolled out their aggressive, war-fighting plans, there were only a few brave souls in Congress and the media who dared to question forthrightly the usefulness of those plans. In 2002 Congress passed legislation giving Bush broad leeway to launch a war against Iraq, and in 2004 the country's still high level of fearfulness helped give an electoral victory to Bush as the country's "wartime leader."

By November 2006, something had changed. Bush's aura as a wartime leader had faded, overtaken by the facts of his administration's deep incompetence—in Iraq, in New Orleans, and elsewhere. It had become clear that our country's possession and use of overwhelming military power had not won the counterterrorist gains Bush had promised, either in Iraq or Afghanistan. And, as the CCGA poll data indicated, many Americans no longer bought the rhetoric about the need for perpetual U.S. supremacy, self-centeredness, and unilateralism.

So now, we have a good basis on which to start building a foreign policy grounded more in a sense of hope and possibility than in a continuation of fear. The possibilities for what all of humanity can achieve, if we all work together over the years ahead to address our many remaining challenges, are truly awe-inspiring. We *can* find ways to ease the tensions in the Middle East, bring down the levels of all the forms of armament that make our world such a terrifying place, unlock the massive human potential still held back by grinding poverty in Africa and elsewhere, find politically workable ways of bringing down the world's total CO_2 emissions, and more—but only if we Americans are able to sit down in a spirit of equality and friendliness with the other peoples of the world, and start listening to, and engaging with, their concerns.

That is what global inclusion is all about. It is about working alongside the world's other peoples to deal with common challenges, and reconnecting with that strongly American spirit of hope for the future.

Finally, regarding action, this book will not have served its purpose if, having gotten this far, you, the reader, merely say, "Uh huh, interesting," and put it down. It will be effective only if you find some of the information and ideas here useful—and then you go out and use them.

The interests in our economy and society that support the control paradigm have been in the driver's seat in this country for a long time. Remember, President Eisenhower was warning about the dangers of "the military-industrial complex" fifty years ago! Today, the interests keeping the control paradigm in place stretch far beyond the military-industrial sector to include big carbon, big agribusiness, and more. By pressing their respective cases effectively over past decades, these interests have succeeded in (1) amassing considerable wealth and power, some of which they reinvested in lobbying efforts aimed at keeping their interests dominant on the national agenda, and (2) keeping the discourse in the national media quite tightly within their own, self-serving frames of reference.

But now, a confluence of new developments—the wide recognition of the folly of invading Iraq and the limitations on the usefulness of raw military power, awareness of the urgency of dealing with global warming, and the deep shifts in the international power balance—have brought our country to a turning point. A broad array of organizations is working on the issues discussed in this book. I shall put the contact details for some of these into my Resource section—but there are many others, too. Also, in line with the broad theme of inclusiveness, the kinds of citizen actions these challenges require are not limited to any one political party.

How can we all work together to reconnect the deep human wisdom so many Americans already bring to their consideration of international issues with the actual policies of our leaders? Global includers will need to organize a spirited campaign in every congressional district and at a broader level, too. We can network with friends and neighbors, with our congregations and the broader denominations to which they belong, with civic groups, and with the national headquarters or local branches of activist and information-providing organizations like those listed in the Resource section. We can organize local informational meetings, letter-writing campaigns, or a host of other nonviolent civic actions. We certainly should make our views known to legislators and all candidates for electoral office in a variety of ways, and we should work hard to persuade them to adopt as many items on the global inclusion agenda as possible. Some readers may want to focus on one or two items on the agenda. Others may want to address it more broadly. We need to work hard to get the ideas of global inclusion discussed and endorsed at every level, and to press for a foreign policy informed by them.

In each of the chapters of this book, I have suggested the kinds of specific policies for which global includers should press. You and your friends probably have suggestions and ideas of your own. (I hope you do!) Also, the details of the policies we want to push forward may change somewhat over time. But here, as a general guide, is a top ten list of the broad principles global includers would advocate, for our country's foreign policy. The United States should:

1. Recommit, in deeds and words, to the American ideals of human equality, fairness, respect, and generosity.
2. Invest the time needed to assess the effects of our policies on other people around the world, and *stop or reverse those policies that harm* other peoples, even as we *increase the help* we give them.
3. Join and commit strongly to the many international agreements from which in recent years Washington has stood aside or done much to weaken.
4. Brainstorm in a respectful way with people and leaders from other countries, seek out and engage fair-mindedly with their suggestions on how to address the big challenges we all have in common, and remember that Americans do not have all the answers—and no one really expects us to!
5. Cut back our country's reliance on military power, work with other nations to build everyone's security and reduce the size of military arsenals everywhere, and switch U.S. funds massively from military goods to diplomacy, aid, and other tools that build human security.
6. Engage seriously with other countries in planning how to make good on the long-standing pledge of the NPT for a world free of all nuclear weapons, and commit to following those plans.
7. Look at fairness issues in international trade, not just aid, and make trade fair and aid generous and effective.
8. Work for the full spectrum of human rights at home and abroad: that means social and economic rights as well as civil and political rights.
9. Strengthen the United Nations and all other nonmilitary international bodies.
10. Work actively and fair-mindedly with other nations to deal with global warming.

There are many ways that we can all, as Americans, start to make global inclusion a reality, and not just a dream: a reality for our people and for the 6 billion humans elsewhere, too. Today, we are all in this fragile boat of human survival together. Let's work together to steer it onto a safe course—and let us celebrate and learn from all the new human connections we can make along the way.

Resources for Global Re-Engagement: Action and Topics Toolkits

This appendix is organized in two parts. First, there is an Action Toolkit that points you toward some of the best resources available for planning different kinds of action around the issues discussed in this book. The second part, the Topics Toolkit, points toward good resources for information and activism.

Action Toolkit

If you want to start taking action on the issues covered in this book but are not sure where or how to start, one good place to begin is your public library. Library staff will be happy to help you identify local organizations involved in the issues you want to work on. (Networking with existing organizations is generally much easier than starting out from scratch.) If you do not have computer access elsewhere, the library computers will give you access to all the materials listed here that are available only online. If you and your friends are planning informational events, a library can either provide you with a meeting room on their premises or help you find one elsewhere, and most libraries will post notices about the events you plan. Finally, a library is also a great place to borrow all the books you want to read!

You will find some helpful activity organizing suggestions at the following websites:

Friends Committee on National Legislation, *Grassroots Toolkit:* www.fcnl.org/action/toolkit.htm. Solid information on how to lobby Congress and do community and media outreach.

Global Exchange, *How to Organize!* www.codepink4peace.org/downloads/howtoorganizetoolkit.pdf. This twenty-page PDF file can be printed and has straightforward "how-to's" on meeting with legislators and keeping in touch with them, holding issue-based house parties, organizing different kinds of demonstrations, media outreach, and more.

Student PIRGs *Activist Toolkit,* www.studentpirgs.org/toolkit.asp. The left sidebar has links to excellent "how-to" pages on organizing meetings, doing media outreach, and strategic planning. The site is focused on student activism, but most of the resources here are useful in any context.

Tipping Point Strategies, *Toolbox,* www.tippingpointstrategies.org/toolbox.html. This toolbox is for people and groups working to improve their online organizing. The first blog listed has good information, as does the slide show at the bottom.

Training for Change, *Tools,* trainingforchange.org/content/section/4/39. Great ideas for team-building in the context of any campaign for nonviolent change. Good for social change groups both old and brand new!

U.S. in the World, *Talking Global Issues with Americans: A Practical Guide,* www.gii-exchange.org/guide. If you don't feel self-confident enough to discuss global issues with your neighbors, this site can give you helpful tips on how to get started.

Vancouver Citizen's Committee, *The Citizen's Handbook,* www.vcn.bc.ca/citizens-handbook. From north of the border, excellent tips on organizing community-based campaigns. The first section, "Community Organizing," is particularly useful.

Virginia Organizing Project, *Organizing Toolbox,* virginia-organizing.org/toolbox.php. Scroll down for links to around forty informative articles. Focused on state-level action in Virginia but easily adaptable to other contexts.

Topics Toolkit

Under each of the headings that follows, the sources cited in the book give much more information than was referenced there and are worth consulting in full. I have generally not included them here. Check the Notes section instead.

In the lists of organizations, I have tagged each entry with its strengths. These tags are:

A = Activism
P = Print information
W = Web-based information

Many of the texts listed below as "web-based resources" are also available in print form. Usually, the website gives information about ordering the print version.

Security, War, and Peace

Organizations

Center for Arms Control and Non-Proliferation
322 Fourth Street, NE
Washington, DC 20002
www.armscontrolcenter.org
W Good online materials on many security issues including U.S. defense budgeting.

Crisis Group
1629 K St., NW, Suite 450
Washington, DC 20006
www.crisisgroup.org
P,W Timely reports on the world's key crisis zones—full texts available on the Web and in print.

Federation of American Scientists
1725 DeSales St., NW, 6th Fl.
Washington, DC 20036
www.fas.org
A,W Broad resources on WMDs at www.fas.org/nuke. Check their great Strategic Security Blog: www.fas.org/blog/ssp.

Friends Committee on National Legislation
245 Second Street NE
Washington, DC 20002
www.fcnl.org
A,W Quaker-based FCNL lobbies Congress on war and peace issues, and provides many good resources especially on peaceful prevention of violent conflict.

Stockholm International Peace Research Institute
Signalistgatan 9

SE-169 70
Solna, Sweden
www.sipri.org
P,W Publishes an important yearbook on war and peace. Its Web-based resources are good but do not include the yearbook.

United for Peace and Justice
P.O. Box 607
Times Square Stn.
New York, NY 10108
www.unitedforpeace.org
A,W The largest nationwide coalition of antiwar organizations. Its resources are activism-focused.

Web-based Resources

Most U.S. government agencies, including the White House, the Departments of State and Defense, and the Senate and House Committees on Armed Services and Foreign Relations, have good websites offering important primary source material. The Special Inspector General for Iraq Reconstruction has an informative site: www.sigir.mil. Many UN websites are informative, including, on nuclear proliferation issues, that of the International Atomic Energy Agency (IAEA), www.iaea.org. There are many sites expressing vigorous views for and against Washington's current wars. The following sites offer notably useful and solid information.

Anup Shah, "Geopolitics" section of his *Global Issues* website, at www.globalissues.org/Geopolitics. Shah's site is informative, with many helpful links. It also has big sections on the topics of the other chapters here, and is worth exploring.

Council on Foreign Relations, *"Dirty bombs,"* info sheet at www.cfr.org/publication/9548. Check out the rest of CFR's website, too.

International Committee of the Red Cross, *The People on War Report* (2000), full text available as a PDF at http://icrc.org/web/eng/siteeng0.nsf/htmlall/p0758. A great grassroots view of war, presenting the attitudes and experiences of people from twelve war-torn countries.

Juan Cole, *Informed Comment,* at www.juancole.com, is mainly about Iraq. The associated group blog, *Informed Comment: Global Affairs* (icga.blogspot.com), has good writers on Afghanistan and Iran.

Project on Defense Alternatives: www.comw.org/pda. This site has well-informed analysis on defense issues and helpful links to other sources. Check out particularly the buttons for "War Report" (news and analysis on Iraq and Afghanistan), "Chinese Military Power," and "Occupation Distress."

UN Commission on Human Security, *Final Report of the Commission on Human Security* (2003), in seven languages, at www.humansecurity-chs.org/finalreport/index.html.

War Resisters League, *Where Your Income Tax Dollars Really Go,* pie chart published annually to show distribution of U.S. governmental spending, at www.warresisters.org/piechart.htm.

Books

Andrew J. Bacevich, *American Empire: The Realities and Consequences of U.S. Diplomacy* (Cambridge: Harvard University Press, 2002).

Richard Rhodes, *Arsenals of Folly: The Making of the Nuclear Arms Race* (New York: Random House, 2007).

Thomas E. Ricks, *Fiasco: The American Military Adventure in Iraq* (New York: Penguin, 2006).

"Riverbend," *Baghdad Burning: Girl Blog from Iraq* (New York: Feminist Press at the City University of New York, 2005).

Rupert Smith, *The Utility of Force: The Art of War in the Modern World* (London: Penguin, 2005). You can read a good interview with Smith online at icrc.org/web/eng/siteeng0.nsf/htmlall/review-864-p719.

Ramesh Thakur, *The United Nations, Peace and Security* (Cambridge, UK: Cambridge, 2006).

Inequality, Trade, and Aid

Organizations

New Rules for Global Finance
2200 Wilson Blvd., Suite 650
Arlington, VA 22201
www.new-rules.org
A Group dedicated to reforming decision-making in the World Bank and IMF.

Oxfam America
226 Causeway St., 5th Fl.
Boston, MA 02114
www.oxfamamerica.org

A,P,W Part of the global 'Oxfam' network, working in development projects around the world. Oxfam also does good advocacy work on global economic issues, including the "Make Trade Fair" campaign, and offers great resources to back this up.

Third World Network
131, Jalan Macalister
10400, Penang
Malaysia
www.twnside.org.sg

P,W Network of economists and social activists from low-income countries analyzing the WTO and other global issues.

Web-based Resources

The World Bank, the International Monetary Fund, and the Organization for Economic Cooperation and Development all have well-organized websites with lots of excellent statistics and information on them. (The World Trade Organization's site is puny and outdated.) The United Nations has many informative websites on global economics. Check in particular:

- hdr.undp.org, for the *Human Development Report* published annually by the UN Development Program offering full texts, statistical tables, and many excellent statistical and mapping tools;
- www.un.org/millenniumgoals, official site for the Millennium Development Goals;
- www.irinnews.org, which has in-depth news of social and economic affairs in many low-income countries; and
- www.wider.unu.edu, site of the UN-affiliated World Institute for Development Economics Research.

Ken Cook, *Mulch*. Blog from the president of the Environmental Working Group, with much data about U.S. farm subsidies: www.mulchblog.com.

Ann Cullen, "How Europe Wrote the Rules of Global Finance: Q&A with Rawi E. Abdelal," on Harvard Business School Working Knowledge site at hbswk.hbs.edu/item/5475.html.

National Cotton Council of America website, at www.cotton.org.

Thomas Pogge, "World Poverty and Human Rights" (PDF), on Carnegie Council site at www.cceia.org/resources/journal/19_1/symposium/5109.html.

Rami Zurayk, *Land and People*. Lively blog on "food, farming, and rural society" written by an agronomist at the American University of Beirut. Deals with issues in the global agricultural economy as well as local agricultural and ecological themes. Available at landandpeople.blogspot.com.

Books

Paul Collier, *The Bottom Billion: Why the Poorest Countries Are Failing and What Can Be Done about It* (New York: Oxford University Press, 2007).

Jeffrey D. Sachs, *The End of Poverty: Economic Possibilities for Our Time* (New York: Penguin, 2006).

Joseph E. Stiglitz, *Globalization and Its Discontents* (New York: W. W. Norton, 2003).

Joseph E. Stiglitz, *Making Globalization Work* (New York: W. W. Norton, 2007).

Human Rights

Organizations

American Civil Liberties Union
125 Broad St., 18th Fl.
New York, NY 10004
www.aclu.org
A,P,W ACLU works against U.S. torture and other detention abuses. The website also has good materials on rights aspects of the Hurricane Katrina events.

Amnesty International (USA)
5 Penn Plaza, 14th Fl.
New York, NY 10001
www.amnesty.org
A,P,W Membership-based global rights network. AI runs campaigns and does good documentation. Check the "Library" tab on their website.

Center for Constitutional Rights
666 Broadway, 7th Fl.
New York, NY 10012
ccrjustice.org
A,W Does important work on Guantánamo and rights issues inside the United States.

Human Rights First
333 Seventh Ave., 13th Fl.

New York, NY 10001
www.humanrightsfirst.org
A,W Lawyer-based activist organization with strong projects on torture and Iraqi refugees.

Human Rights Watch
350 Fifth Ave, 34th Fl.
New York, NY 10118
hrw.org
A,P,W Runs campaigns and publishes many topical reports.

International Committee of the Red Cross
ICRC Regional Delegation
1100 Connecticut Ave., Suite 500
Washington, DC 20036
icrc.org/eng
P,W The "guardian" organization for the Geneva and Hague conventions. The site has great materials on International Humanitarian Law (IHL).

Web-based Resources

Cageprisoners. Informative site based in the United Kingdom that advocates for the rights of Guantánamo prisoners and their families: www.cageprisoners.com.

Center for Economic and Social Rights (New York), Basic Primer, at cesr.org/basic.

Century Foundation, Afghanistan Watch blog: www.afghanistanwatch.org.

University of Minnesota, Human Rights Library. Excellent, easily searchable documentation in eight languages, www1.umn.edu/humanrts.

UN Office of the High Commissioner for Human Rights: www.ohchr.org/english. Lots of documentation, and news and reports on the actions (and inactions) of the United Nations on rights issues.

Books

Roy Gutman and David Rieff, *Crimes of War: What the Public Should Know* (New York: W. W. Norton, 1999).

Joseph Margulies, *Guantánamo and the Abuse of Presidential Power* (New York: Simon and Schuster, 2007).

Resources for Global Re-Engagement • 119

Amartya Sen, *Development as Freedom* (New York: Anchor Books, 1999).

H. C. von Sponeck, *A Different Kind of War: The UN Sanctions Regime in Iraq* (Oxford, UK: Berghahn Books, 2006).

Climate Change

Organizations

Christian Aid
P.O. Box 100
London, UK SE1 7RT
www.christianaid.org.uk
A,P,W Has terrific online and print resources for its campaign for worldwide climate justice.

Greenpeace USA
702 H St., NW
Washington, DC 20001
www.greenpeace.org/usa
A,W U.S. branch of veteran global network of environmental activists. Also check the resources available at www.greenpeace.org/international.

Natural Resources Defense Council
40 West 20th St.
New York, NY 10011
nrdc.org
A,W Website has good sections on green living, nuclear weapons, and more.

Union of Concerned Scientists
2 Brattle Sq.
Cambridge, MA 02238
www.ucsusa.org
A,P,W Very informative website.

Web-based Resources

The U.S. government publishes statistics on CO_2 emissions in two key places: www.eia.doe.gov/emeu/international/carbondioxide.html and cdiac.esd.ornl.gov. Various UN-related bodies have informative websites on climate issues. These include:

- UN Environment Program, at www.unep.org. Also, many great UNEP-related graphics are available at maps.grida.no.
- UN Framework Convention on Climate Change, at unfccc.int.
- UN Intergovernmental Panel on Climate Change (cowinner of the 2007 Nobel Peace Prize) at www.ipcc.ch. Sections of the important IPCC Fourth Assessment Report (2007) are also available in print.

Ethan Arpi et al., The City Fix. Blog on urban mobility systems and sustainability at embarqblog.wri.org.

Pew Center on Global Climate Change. Informative and well-organized site at www.pewclimate.org. Good section on "China and Climate Change."

Terra Daily: News about Planet Earth. News aggregator at www.terradaily.com.

"The Threat of Climate Change," *Washington Post* aggregator for news reports and analysis on the climate issue, including several good graphics, tinyurl.com/flsk3.

UK government, "Stern Review on the Economics of Climate Change." Full text, executive summary (in fifteen languages), and other materials, available at tinyurl.com/vgzxv. Also available as print version.

World Wildlife Fund, "Living Planet Report 2006." Beautiful and informative forty-four-page report available in ten languages at www.panda.org/news_facts/publications/living_planet_report/lp_2006.

Books

Elizabeth Economy, *The River Runs Black: The Environmental Challenge to China's Future* (Ithaca, NY: Cornell University Press, 2004).

Kerry Emanuel, *What We Know about Climate Change* (Cambridge: Massachusetts Institute of Technology Press, 2007).

Al Gore, *An Inconvenient Truth* (New York: Rodale Books, 2006). Also, the Oscar-winning movie version.

Robert Henson, *The Rough Guide to Climate Change* (London: Rough Guides, 2006).

Elizabeth Kolbert, *Field Notes from a Catastrophe: Man, Nature, and Climate Change* (New York: Bloomsbury, 2006).

Wolfgang Sachs and Tilman Santarius, eds., *Fair Future: Resource Conflicts, Security and Global Justice* (London: Zed Books, 2005).

Global Relationships

Organizations

Global Policy Forum
777 UN Plaza, Suite 3D
New York, NY 10017
www.globalpolicy.org
A,W Monitors the United Nations and the global financial institutions, among other projects.

UN Association of the USA
801 Second Ave., 2nd Fl.
New York, NY 10017
www.unausa.org
A,P,W Advocates for stronger U.S. support of the United Nations, organizes local chapters, and publishes informative quarterly, *The InterDependent*.

Web-based Resources

Aspen Institute, U.S. in the World: Talking Global Issues with Americans at www.gii-exchange.org/guide. (Interesting, if slightly bossy, guide to discussing these topics with friends and colleagues.)

Institute for Policy Studies, Foreign Policy in Focus at www.fpif.org.

Tim Johnson, China Rises at washingtonbureau.typepad.com/china. Well-written blog by McClatchy's bureau chief in Beijing describes daily life and policy issues in China and its neighbors. (See also the blogs written by McClatchy staff in other countries, linked to on China Rises.)

NationMaster at www.nationmaster.com. Great tool for retrieving and displaying comparative statistics about different countries' performance in many fields.

People's Daily Online, Sino-US Relations in the Eyes of Chinese: Survey at tinyurl.com/34p7jf. Revealing survey conducted in five Chinese cities in 2005. The rest of this English-language website is also worth exploring at english.peopledaily.com.cn.

Program on International Policy Attitudes, WorldPublicOpinion at worldpublicopinion.org. Excellent, well-organized site.

Books

Zbigniew Brzezinski, *The Choice: Global Domination or Global Leadership* (New York: Basic Books, 2004).

Josef Joffe, *Überpower: The Imperial Temptation of America* (New York: W. W. Norton, 2007).

Jackie Smith et al., *Global Democracy and the World Social Forums* (Boulder, CO: Paradigm Publishers, 2007).

Stephen M. Walt, *Taming American Power: The Global Response to U.S. Primacy* (New York: W. W. Norton, 2005).

Notes

Note to Chapter 1

1. These are among the many important findings of the *Fourth Assessment Report* released in early 2007 by the UN Intergovernmental Panel on Climate Change—the body that shared the 2007 Nobel Peace Prize with Al Gore. You can access the various sections of this report online at http://ipcc-wg1.ucar.edu/wg1/wg1-report.html.

Notes to Chapter 2

1. Part III of the "National Security Strategy of the United States of America" (Washington DC: The White House, September 2002). Accessed at http://www.whitehouse.gov/nsc/nss3.html, 9/18/07.

2. "Fatalities from Terrorist Attacks, 1908–2004," National Consortium for the Study of Terrorism and Responses to Terrorism, at http://209.232.239.37/gtd2/charts/fatalities.gif. For 2005–2006, U.S. State Department National Counterterrorism Center, Annex of Statistical Information, April 30, 2007, at http://www.state.gove/s/ct/ns/crt/2006/82739.htm.

3. From UN General Assembly resolution 51/210, "Measures to Eliminate International Terrorism," 1999.

4. Figures from "Country Reports on Terrorism 2006," issued by the State Department Office of the Coordinator for Counterterrorism, April 2007. Accessed at http://www.state.gov/s/ct/rls/crt/2006/82739.htm, 9/18/07.

5. Karen DeYoung and Walter Pincus, "Al-Qaeda's Gains Keep U.S. at Risk, Report Says," *Washington Post,* July 18, 2007, A1.

6. See Hans M. Kristenson, "White House Guidance Led to New Nuclear Strike Plans against Proliferators, Document Shows," on the Federation of American Scientists' Strategic Security Blog, November 5, 2007, accessed

11/20/07 at http://www.fas.org/blog/ssp/2007/11/white_house_guidance_led_to_ne.php.

7. See IRIN, "Small Arms: The Real Weapons of Mass Destruction," available at http://www.irinnews.org/IndepthMain.aspx?IndepthId=8&ReportId=58952.

8. Calculated from *The Military Balance 2007* (London: IISS, 2007), 406–411.

9. *The Military Balance 2007* (London: IISS, 2007), 412.

10. "New Dimensions of Human Security," *Human Development Report 1994* (New York: UN Development Program, 1994), ch. 2, 1–2.

11. Sam Nunn, "The Mountaintop: A World Free of Nuclear Weapons." Text of a speech given at the Council on Foreign Relations, June 14, 2007. Accessed 10/25/07 at http://www.nti.org/c_press/speech_samnunn_cfr07.pdf.

Notes to Chapter 3

1. The defense budget figure is from *Military Balance 2007* (London: IISS, 2007), 406; the ODA figures are from the OECD website at http://www.oecd.org/dataoecd/52/18/37790990.pdf.

2. OECD report on "Final ODA data for 2005," accessed 8/8/07 at http://www.oecd.org/dataoecd/52/18/37790990.pdf.

3. Chart "IBRD [i.e., World Bank] Executive Directors Voting Status," accessed 8/7/07 at http://go.worldbank.org/3QYBPQLR50; and chart "IMF Executive Directors and Voting Power," accessed at http://www.imf.org/external/np/sec/memdir/eds.htm.

4. Branko Milanovic, *Worlds Apart: Measuring International and Global Inequality* (Princeton, NJ: Princeton University Press, 2005), 63–70.

5. Branko Milanovic, *Worlds Apart: Measuring International and Global Inequality* (Princeton and Oxford: Princeton University Press, 2005), Table 10.2.

6. Kevin Watkins, *Rigged Rules and Double Standards: Trade, Globalization, and the Fight against Poverty* (Oxford, UK: Oxfam, 2002), 5.

7. Environmental Working Group Farm Subsidy Database. Accessed 7/8/07 at http://farm.ewg.org/sites/farm/regionsummary.php?fips=00000.

8. Environmental Working Group Farm Subsidy Database, accessed at http://farm.ewg.org/sites/farm/regionsummary.php?fips=00000.

9. BBC, "U.S. Loses Cotton Subsidies Fight." Accessed 10/26/07 at http://news.bbc.co.uk/2/hi/business/7046195.stm.

10. G. Pascal Zachary, "100% Rotten," published on the CNN-Money website, December 1, 2005. Accessed 8/9/07 at http://money.cnn.com/magazines/business2/business2_archive/2005/12/01/8364585/index.htm.

11. *Rigged Rules*, 8.

12. OECD, *2006 Survey on Monitoring the Paris Declaration, Overview of the Results: Pre-Publication Copy* (Paris: OECD, 2007), Table B.8: "How Much Aid Is Untied? Accessed at http://www.oecd.org/dataoecd/0/45/38597363.pdf, 86.

Note to Chapter 4

1. All data are from the UNDP's *Human Development Report 2006*, except those for political rights and civil liberties, which were derived from the Freedom House Indicators (F) using the formula $X = 115 - 15 \cdot F$.

Notes to Chapter 5

1. "IPCC, 2007: Summary for Policymakers." In *Climate Change 2007: The Physical Science Basis—Contribution of Working Group I to the Fourth Assessment Report of the Intergovernmental Panel on Climate Change*, S. Solomon, D. Qin, M. Manning, Z. Chen, M. Marquis, K. B. Averyt, M. Tignor, and H. L. Miller (eds.) (Cambridge, UK, and New York: Cambridge University Press, 2007). Accessed 8/21/2007 at http://ipcc-wg1.ucar.edu/wg1/Report/AR4WG1_Pub_SPM-v2.pdf, 2, 3, 6 (Figure SPM.3), and 8 (Table SPM.2).

2. U.S. Energy Information Administration, International Energy Annual 2004. (The figures for the "EU-25" group were derived from those given for all of Europe, by subtracting Turkey and some smaller non-EU countries.)

3. More information is available from http://www.ucsusa.org/clean_energy/clean_energy_policies/res-at-work-in-the-states.html.

4. Oxfam, *Adapting to Climate Change: What's Needed in Poor Countries and Who Should Pay* (Oxford: Oxfam, May 2007), 2.

5. Douglas V. Johnson II, *Global Climate Change: National Security Implications* (Carlisle, PA: U.S. Army War College Strategic Studies Institute, May 2007), p. 1.

6. Nicholas Stern, "Stern Review: The Economics of Climate Change," Executive Summary, p. xxvii. Accessed 8/23/07 at http://www.hm-treasury.gov.uk/media/4/3/Executive_Summary.pdf.

7. See the English-language slide presentation by Chinese official Gao Guangsheng on the antiwarming policy adopted by the government in June 2007. Accessed 11/1/07 at www.pewclimate.org/docUploads/Gao%20Guangsheng.pdf.

8. U.S. Energy Information Administration, *International Energy Annual, 2004*.

9. See Paul Baer, Tom Athanasiou, and Sivan Kartha, "The Right to Development in a Climate Constrained World." Accessed 11/1/07 at http://www.ecoequity.org/docs/TheGDRsFramework.pdf.

Notes to Chapter 6

1. IMF World Economic Outlook Database (Washington, DC: International Monetary Fund, April 2007 Edition). Accessed 9/4/07 through http://www.imf.org/external/pubs/ft/weo/2007/01/data/weoseglr.aspx.

2. IMF World Economic Outlook Database (Washington, DC: International Monetary Fund, April 2007 Edition). Accessed 9/4/07 through http://www.imf.org/external/pubs/ft/weo/2007/01/data/weoseglr.aspx.

3. Condoleezza Rice, "Campaign 2000: Promoting the National Interest," *Foreign Affairs* (January–February 2000). Accessed 8/31/07 at http://www.foreignaffairs.org/20000101faessay5/condoleezza-rice/campaign-2000-promoting-the-national-interest.html.

4. Chicago Council on Global Affairs and WorldPublicOpinion.org, "World Publics Reject U.S. Role as the World Leader," polling conducted July–December 2006. Accessed 9/11/2007 at http://worldpublicopinion.org/ind/printable_version.php?pnt=345.

5. Kishore Mahbubani, *Beyond the Age of Innocence: Rebuilding Trust between America and the World* (New York: Public Affairs, 2005), 165–166.

6. WorldPublicOpinion.org, "Comprehensive Analysis of Polls Reveals Americans' Attitudes on U.S. Role in the World," August 3, 2007. Accessed 9/11/07 at http://www.americans-world.org/digest/overview/us_role/usrole_summary.cfm.

Index

Abbott, Chris, 5, 6
Abu Ghraib, 68, 89
Action Toolkit, contents of, 111–112
Adaptation measures, 81–82
Afghanistan, U.S. presence in, 55, 56, 59
African National Congress, 62
Agribusiness, 47, 104
Aid, 27, 38, 115–117; increase in, 96; to low-income countries, 49; military, 103; to poor, 48; revitalizing, 48; from some rich countries, 39 (fig.); U.S. internal constraints on, 48–49; wise use of, 47–49
Al-Qaeda, 2, 22, 54, 86; attacking, 55, 56
American Civil Liberties Union (ACLU), 117
Amnesty International, 54, 117
Annan, Kofi, 1
Anti-Land Mine Treaty, 34
Antiwarming campaign, 80, 83
Apartheid, 62
AQI, 13
Arab-Israeli conflict, 5
Armed Services Committee, 28
Arms market, 29; countries' shares of, 30 (fig.)
Arms race, 33, 65; cessation of, 27
Article 6 of Nuclear Nonproliferation Treaty, 27, 34
Atrocities, 58, 60, 66, 67
Aum Shinrikyo, 24

Bali negotiation, 76, 80
Ballistic missile defense system, 28
Beyond Terror: The Truth about the Real Threats to Our World (Abbott, Roger, and Sloboda), 5
Bin Laden, Osama, 55
Biofuels, 79
Biological weapons, 24
Bush, George W.: control paradigm and, 6, 19; democracy and, 89; diplomacy and, 90; economic decline and, 89; environmental issues and, 72, 80, 86; international affairs and, 6, 8, 13; Iraq invasion and, 2, 3–4, 12, 54, 86, 106–107; Kyoto Protocol and, 72, 90; military budget and, 28; National Security Strategy document of, 31; September 11 and, 19, 55; unilateralism of, 102

"Cap and trade" schemes, 77
Carbon dependence, 75, 76, 77, 82, 83
Carbon dioxide, 74, 75, 76, 79, 82, 83; converging U.S./China emissions of, 81 (fig.); by countries/groupings, 71 (fig.); emissions of per head,

71; reducing, 72, 77, 78; in United States, 70
CCGA. *See* Chicago Council of Global Affairs
CDM. *See* Clean Development Mechanism
Center for Arms Control and Non-Proliferation, 113
Center for Constitutional Rights, 117
Central Intelligence Agency (CIA), 56
CFCs, 70
Challenges, 8–12, 19–25, 27–34, 80, 109; re-engaging with, 9, 13–14; threats and, 8–9
Chemical weapons, 24
Cheney, Richard: energy policy and, 80
Chicago Council of Global Affairs (CCGA), 93, 94, 96, 107
Child mortality, reducing, 50
Children's rights, 63–64
China: economic growth in, 81, 86; energy efficiency in, 81; global warming and, 98; human rights in, 64; nuclear power in, 79; Olympics in, 99; rise of, 91, 97, 98, 99; WTO and, 91
Christian Aid, 82, 119
Christian Science Monitor, vi, 4
Civil rights, 63, 64, 66
Clean Development Mechanism (CDM), 72, 80
Climate change, 2, 69, 74, 119–120; adaptation to, 75; challenge of, 11–12, 80, 83; impact of, 70
Clinton, Bill, 58, 90; economic surplus and, 89; Kyoto Protocol and, 72; Rwandan genocide and, 59
Cold War, 5, 23, 27, 90, 92
Communist Party, 97; Chinese wealth and, 99
Comprehensive Test Ban Treaty, 34
Conference on Disarmament, 33
Conflict: atrocities and, 66; avoiding, 18, 33; intergroup, 67
Connectedness, v, 10, 54, 104, 109, 110
Control paradigm, 19, 102, 106, 107; global inclusion and, 5–8; retaining, 97
Cooperation, 51; negotiated, 102
Crisis Group, 113
Cuba, sanctions against, 58
Cultural Revolution, 64, 99

Darfur, 55, 74, 92
Debt, 51, 97; cutting burden of, 49; foreigners and, 86
Declaration of Independence, 10
Decolonization, 4, 97
Democracy, spread of, 89
Democratic Republic of Congo (DRC): human rights abuses in, 55; human security and, 60
Desertification, 74
Developing countries: cooperation with, 51; debt problems for, 51
Development partnerships, 51
Dignity, 36, 53
Diplomacy, 29, 90, 109; funding for, 33; golden-rule, 104; intelligent, 63; quiet, 58, 63–66
Dirty bombs, 24
Dobriansky, Paula, 76, 80
Drinking water, providing for, 50

Earth Summit, 83
Economic crises, 10, 40
Economic governance, 52, 105
Economic growth, 83, 96; in China, 81, 86; in India, 86
Economic performance: of some nations/regions, 88 (fig.); United States/China compared, 87, 87 (fig.)
Economic power, 12; decline of, 89; military power and, 87, 88
Economic rights, 63, 64, 66, 97, 104, 107, 109
Education, 50
Eisenhower, Dwight D., 85
El-Baradei, Mohammed, 34
Engagement: constructive, 58, 65; rules of, 91

Environmental issues, 11, 72, 73, 74, 80, 105; addressing, 96
Environmental Protection Agency, national effort and, 78
Environmental sustainability, 50; challenge of, 11–12
Environmental Working Group, 45
European Union (EU), 12, 42; expansion of, 86; IMF and, 40; WTO and, 45–46

Failed states, preventing emergence of, 21
Failed States Index, 21
FCNL. See Friends Committee on National Legislation
Federation of American Scientists, 113
Foreign policy, 103, 109
Foreign Relations Committee, 28
Fossil fuels, alternatives to, 79
Freedom, 53, 65
Friends Committee on National Legislation (FCNL), vii, 111, 113
Fund for Peace, 21
Future, planning for, 74–77

Gao Guangsheng, 125n6
Gender equality, promoting, 50
General Agreement on Tariffs and Trade (GATT), 41
Geneva Conventions, 64, 89, 95, 106
Global community, 3, 44, 52; role in, 14
Global economy, 10, 43, 44; China and, 86; control approach and, 52; income distributions in, 43 (fig.)
Global Environmental Fund (GEF), 82
Global Exchange, 111–112
Global inclusion, 9–10, 32, 34, 51–52, 54, 68, 77, 102, 106, 107, 108–109; control and, 5–8; foreign policy of, 7–8, 103; future of, 110; global New Deal and, 52; global warming and, 70; sustainable economy and, 12; trade and, 39–40; weapons proliferation and, 30, 33; world power and, 98

Globalization, 38, 39, 95; inequality and, 42–49
Global Policy Forum, 120–121
Global power: balance of, 7, 12, 91, 98; shifts in, 86, 97–98
Global warming, vii, 75, 76, 78, 83, 102; burdens of, 73–74; carbon dioxide–based, 82; challenge of, 11, 109; China and, 98; contributing to, 70; global includers and, 70; reducing, 12, 13, 73, 82
Global War on Terrorism (GWOT), 19, 89
Good governance, 51
Gore, Al, 11, 78, 123n1
Great Society, 48
Greenhouse gases, 69, 70, 98; reducing, 71, 72, 73, 75
Green Party, 74
Greenpeace USA, 119
Green Revolution, 48
Guantánamo, 68, 89
GWOT. See Global War on Terrorism

Health programs, 40
Heavily Indebted Poor Countries (HIPCs), 51
Helsinki Treaty, 65
Hitler, Adolf, 92
HIV/AIDS, combating, 50
House Agricultural Committee, cotton subsidies and, 47
Humanitarianism, terminology of, 63–64
Human rights, 6, 15, 105, 109, 117–118; action agenda for, 66–68; in China, 64; credibility on, 68; improving, 10, 54, 55, 65, 68; indicators for various countries, 57 (fig.); sustainable, 56; terminology of, 63–64; U.S troops in Afghanistan and, 56
Human rights abuses, 55, 58, 60, 97; challenge of, 10–11; economic sanctions against, 61; end of, 62; victims of, 54

Human Rights First, 117
Human Rights Watch, 5, 54, 117–118
Hunger, eradicating, 50
Hurricane Katrina, 51, 73, 89
Hussein, Saddam, 2, 4, 24, 55, 62; human rights record of, 54; sanctions against, 61; WMDs of, 54

IAEA. *See* International Atomic Energy Agency
ICC. *See* International Criminal Court
ICCPR. *See* International Covenant on Civil and Political Rights
ICESR. *See* International Covenant on Economic and Social Rights
ICRC. *See* International Committee of the Red Cross
IHL. *See* International humanitarian law
IMF. *See* International Monetary Fund
Income distribution, in global economy, 43 (fig.)
Inequality, 10, 36, 115–117; globalization and, 42–49; social, 20; world peace and, 38
Infant mortality, in Mozambique, 36
Interdependence, 102, 104, 106; global humanity and, 96; United States and, 103
Intergovernmental Panel on Climate Change, 70, 123n1
International action, 78, 80–83
International agreements, 90, 109
International Atomic Energy Agency (IAEA), 13, 33, 34
International Committee of the Red Cross (ICRC), 64
International Covenant on Civil and Political Rights, 63
International Covenant on Economic and Social Rights, 63, 66
International Criminal Court (ICC), 67
International humanitarian law (IHL), 64
International Institute for Strategic Studies, vi, 5
International institutions, 33, 96, 105, 106

International law, 20, 63, 90, 96
International legitimacy, 88, 90
International Monetary Fund (IMF), 40, 42; mitigation/adaptation and, 82; structural adjustment and, 44; voting power in, 41 (fig.)
Internet, v, 86
Intervention, v; military, 58–61
Iraq invasion, 2, 3–4, 10, 54, 76, 86, 106–107; military power and, 89–90
Isolationism, 6, 92, 96, 105

Joffe, Josef, 10, 86, 88
Johnson, Douglas V., II: on climate change, 74
Johnson, Lyndon: Great Society and, 48
Jordan, Barbara, 101
JustWorldNews, v, 5, 15

Karzai, Hamid, 56
Kim Jong-il, 27
King, Martin Luther, Jr., 17
Kissinger, Henry: Article 6 and, 34
Knowledge bases/institutions, building on, 48
Kosovo, 59; human rights abuses in, 58
Kurds, United Nations and, 92
Kyoto Protocol, 12, 71–72, 74, 76, 77, 90; expiration of, 75, 80; ratification of, 72

Leadership, 95; environmental, 72; shared, 93–94
Life expectancy, in Mozambique, 36

Maathai, Wangari, 69, 73
Mahbubani, Kishore, 95, 96
Mandela, Nelson, 23
Mao Zedong, Cultural Revolution and, 99
Marshall, George C., 38
Maternal health, improving, 51
McVeigh, Timothy, 67
MDGs. *See* Millennium Development Goals

Middle East: instability in, 3; isolation from, 23; weapons for, 30
Middle East Advisory Committee (Human Rights Watch), vi, 5, 54
Milanovic, Branko, 42, 43
Military power, vii, 31, 104, 106, 107; economic power and, 87, 88; Iraq invasion and, 89–90; multilateral use of, 96; quest for, 105; reliance on, 109; usefulness of, 108
Military spending, 23, 29 (fig.); increase in, 28
Millennium Development Goals (MDGs), 49, 52; list of, 50–51
Mortality rates, 50
Multilateralism, 96
Myanmar: human rights abuses in, 55; sanctions against, 58

National Commission on the U.S. Role in the World, 33
National Cotton Council, 46
National interests, 70; altruism and, 96; citizen-centered, 103–104
National Security Strategy, 19, 31
Native Americans, vi
NATO, Kosovo and, 59
Natural Resources Defense Council (NRDC), 119
Navajo, United Nations and, 92
New Deal, global, 43, 44, 47, 48, 52
Nobel Committee, 11, 34
Nonmilitary toolkit, 61
Nonproliferation, 27, 28, 33
Northern Ireland, peace negotiations in, 23
Nuclear Nonproliferation Treaty (NPT), 25, 31, 109; Article 6 of, 27, 34; nuclear capabilities of signees of, 26 (table)
Nuclear power, in China, 79
Nuclear weapons, 24, 27; no first use of, 25
Nuclear weapons states, 27, 34; Nuclear Nonproliferation Treaty and, 26 (table)

Nunn, Sam: Article 6 and, 34
Nye, Joseph S., Jr., 87

ODA. *See* Overseas Development Aid
Olympics, China and, 99
Opponents, destruction of, 19–20
Organization for Economic Coordination and Development, 49
Organization for the Prohibition of Chemical Weapons, 33
Overseas Development Aid (ODA), 51
Oxfam, 45, 47, 48, 73, 82, 105; report by, 76

Peace, 59–60, 113–115; global inequalities and, 38; negotiations, 23; promoting, 38
Peace churches, vi–vii
Peacemaking, 33, 36, 59, 60
Penn, William, vi
People's Bank of China, U.S. debt and, 86, 97
Perry, William: Article 6 of Nuclear Nonproliferation Treaty and, 34
Persian Gulf, 2, 3, 104
Playing field, leveling, 43, 44–47
Police forces, 22, 60, 94
Political governance, 105
Political process, 23, 36
Political rights, 63, 64, 66
Poverty, 43, 51–52, 107; effects of, 44; eradicating, 50, 51; public environment and, 48; sociopolitical exclusion and, 51
Prodemocracy movement, 65
Progreen activism, 72
Proliferation: horizontal, 25; vertical, 25, 27, 29
Provincial Reconstruction Teams (PRTs), 56

Radiation devices, 24
Radiological Dispersal Device (RDD), 24
Reciprocity, 90
Reform, inclusive, 52

Regulatory mechanisms, 77
Renewable energy, 72–73; development of, 78; national economy and, 78; questionable, 79
Respect, building, 105
Rice, Condoleezza, 66, 90
Rogers, Paul, 5
Roosevelt, Eleanor, 53
Roosevelt, Franklin D., 45; IMF and, 40; international affairs and, 92; leadership of, 95; United Nations and, 91
Rwandan genocide, 59

Sanctions, 58, 65; impact of, 61, 62–63
Save the Children, 48
Schwarzenegger, Arnold: greenhouse gases and, 72
Sea levels, rising, 73–74
Security, 8, 11, 36, 60, 67, 82, 105, 113–115; border, 74; challenges of, 9–10, 19; considering, 32, 33, 102–103; long-term, 31; people-centered, 103; politically sustainable, 104; state-centered, 103
Self-confidence, 36, 106
Sen, Amartya, 66
September 11, 8, 13, 18; reaction to, 19, 55
Serbia: attack on, 58, 59; sanctions against, 58
Shultz, George: Article 6 and, 34
Sloboda, John, 5
Small arms market, 25, 34
Social rights, 63, 97, 109; importance of, 66; improving, 64
Social safety nets, 95
Social service systems, 44
Soft power, 87, 88–89, 123
South Africa: human security and, 60; peace negotiations in, 23; sanctions against, 58, 62
Space Wars, 28
Stalin, Joseph, 92

Stern, Nicholas, 74, 75, 78, 82
Stockholm International Peace Research Institute, 113
Strategic balance, 28
Strategic triumphalism, 92
Structural adjustments, 18, 40, 44
Student PIRGs, 112
Subsidies, 45; carbon fuel, 77; cotton, 46, 47; recipients of, 46 (fig.)
Sudan: human security and, 60; sanctions against, 58
Suez Canal, 4
Sunday Times (London), 4
Superpowers, 93, 96
Sustainable development, 12, 15; global economy and, 11

Taliban, 22, 55, 56
Tariff barriers, 45, 46
Terrorism, 4; challenge of, 19–23; fatalities from, 20 (fig.)
Terrorists, 9, 56; dealing with, 20, 23; failed states and, 21; isolating/incapacitating, 22; networks of, 21
Threats, challenges and, 8–9
Tibetans, United Nations and, 92
Tipping Point Strategies, 112
Topics Toolkit, 111; contents of, 112–121
Trade, 44, 91, 105, 115–117; global inclusion and, 39–40; industrialized economies and, 39; international, 38, 109; leveling, 42
Training for Change, 112
Truman, Harry S., 92; IMF and, 40; leadership of, 95; United Nations and, 91

Überpower, 10, 86, 88; end of, 90, 91, 97, 98
UDHR. *See* Universal Declaration of Human Rights
Unabomber, 67
UN Association of the USA, 121
UN Charter, 6, 7, 106
UN Children's Fund (UNICEF), 31

UN Development Program (UNDP), 13, 31
UNFCCC. *See* United Nations Framework Convention on Climate Change
UN Framework Convention on Climate Change (UNFCCC), 75
UN General Assembly, 92; human rights and, 63–64; MDGs by, 50–51
UN Human Rights Development Index, 97
UNICEF. *See* United Nations Children's Fund
Unilateralism, 83, 102, 107
Union of Concerned Scientists, 119
United for Peace and Justice, 113–114
United Nations (UN), 2, 3, 5, 13, 31, 56; Cold War and, 92; economic sanctions and, 61, 62; environmental issues and, 80; importance of, 91–93; Kosovo and, 59; peacekeeping and, 59, 60; rights protection and, 58; Rwandan genocide and, 59; strengthening, 109; support for, 105; terrorism and, 20; working through, 96
United States in the World, 112
Universal Declaration of Human Rights (UDHR), 6, 63
UN Security Council, 92, 95; Nuclear Nonproliferation Treaty and, 25
U.S. Army War College, 74
U.S. Department of Agriculture, subsidies from, 45
U.S. State Department, 19; nonmilitary activities by, 28; terrorism and, 21–22

Vancouver Citizen's Committee, 112
Violence, 23, 54; criminal, 9; political, 4

Wall Street Journal, 34
Water treatment, 61
WB. *See* World Bank
Weapons: biological, 24; chemical, 24; nuclear, 24, 25, 27; sales of, 30; U.S. approach to distribution of, 30
Weapons of mass destruction (WMDs), 13, 24, 25, 28, 61; destruction of, 34; false stories of, 54; proliferation of, 19
Weapons proliferation, vii, 19; challenge of, 23–25, 27–34; global includers and, 33; reverse, 27
Wellness indicators, of some countries/groupings, 37 (table)
WMDs. *See* Weapons of mass destruction
Women, empowerment of, 50, 64
World affairs: control over, 32; U.S. role in, 93–96, 94 (fig.), 105
World Bank (WB), 40, 42; mitigation/adaptation and, 82; progreen projects and, 83; voting power in, 41 (fig.)
World Health Organization (WHO), 31
World population, U.S. relationship with, 102–110
WorldPublicOpinion.org, 96, 105
World Trade Organization (WTO), 41–42, 106; China and, 91; cotton subsidies and, 46; European Union and, 45–46; structural adjustments and, 44
WTO. *See* World Trade Organization

Yunus, Muhammad, 35

Zachary, G. Pascal, 46
Zimbabwe: human rights abuses in, 55; sanctions against, 58

About the Author

Helena Cobban is a veteran journalist who has written for the *Christian Science Monitor*, the *Boston Review*, and several other periodicals. She is currently serving as a friend in Washington for the Friends Committee on National Legislation and is author most recently of *Amnesty after Atrocity?* (Paradigm 2006) as well as publisher of justworldnews.org.